PUBLISHED by PARABLES
Earthly Stories with a Heavenly Meaning

OREX JOB K. KOMBEA

THE BIBLICAL BIOLOGY

THE BIOLOGICAL PERSPECTIVES ARE IMPACTED FOR THE BIBLICAL PURPOSES

THE BIOLOGY FULFILLS BIBLE

BY

OREX JOB K. KOMBERG

PUBLISHED by PARABLES
Earthly Stories with a Heavenly Meaning

OREX JOB K. KOMBEA

THE BIBLICAL BIOLOGY
OREX JOB K. KOMBEA

Published By Parables
September, 2020

ISBN 978-1-951497-90-3
Printed in the United States of America

Readers should be aware that Internet Web sites offered as citations and/or sources for further information may have been changed or disappeared between the time this was written and the time it is read.

The Biblical Biology

The Biological Perspectives are Impacted for the Biblical Purposes

The Biology Fulfills Bible

By

Orex Job K. Komberg

PUBLISHED by PARABLES
Earthly Stories with a Heavenly Meaning

OREX JOB K. KOMBEA

FORWARD

This Novel Book was written by Orex Job Kombea, in Lae, Papua New Guinea in 2020. It is known; "The Science of Biological perspectives are impacted for the Biblical purposes". It is quoted with the sufficient biblical referenced knowledge those are corresponding with their chapters and the verses for the philosophy of Science knowledge, especially the biology in excessive dilemmatic dimensions for the lives on earth. The overall examination of the idea is on **empiricism**, meaning that the pursuit of knowledge is through experience by recognition and observation on the functions and operations of the nature in cohered with the general Geographical content knowledge for the biological sciences.

The book is the knowledge-revealing which the relevant sources for the contexts that will be imparted in learning institutions and research scenes. High school level and the Theological institutions are either can be suited for their learning programs, too. There are multi learning areas throughout who can use it as the reference for the integrated knowledge in some diverse contents. The learners and the researchers who use this book can be enabled in enhancing into life moulding. It is also resourceful for the godly people like preachers, pastors, apostles, ministers, teachers, to comprehend their sermons, preaches, speeches and teachings. Collaboratively, they can prove for a complete subject for all circumstances in the means of life on Planet Earth.

Upon the study, the Bible will prove to the Biological Science that the sources of all lives are originated from the Lord God. The science of the biology knowledge expounds for bible knowledge for the Lord God's purpose is what the human being has to come known and understood which is mystery in human understanding.

The main idea about this book focuses on the human biology. Regardless of all other lives on earth, human being is intelligent than other living things. Human being dominates all powers, other living things, and intellectually brilliant in human philosophy. In line with it human being is what operates with common senses. For us to study human being is deep rooted out in physically, spiritually, socially, psychologically, mentally and biologically.

Many a times people (both godly and ungodly) believe and tend to speak out with mouth verbally and orally; the Heaven and the Earth, and everything on them comes from the Lord God, and they are created by him. Yes, biblically it is true. But, how shall we prove to understand that? Now, this book has the answers from the Holy Bible especially for the Science of Biology, like for the other areas known as History, Philosophy, Geography, Prophecy, Poetry, Chemistry, Physics, and Astronomy. The Science of Biology has acquired and lifted up whatever everything in the bible. The intimacy of two approaches (Biological for Biblical) is unjustified through the careful study. The justification of contrary can be the misconception information because the whole approach is thorough empiricism.

The creation and evolution are diverse to each other and contradictory for they are pertaining themselves which each both has the proofs and evidences, that the biblical biology has sufficient embracement that some of us come to know and understand.

Throughout all Science pertaining knowledge in the word of God in the bible is not in the analytical sequence that maybe we ought to understand that easily and discover in the quicker paces. They are scattered all over the place in both the Old and the New Testaments. We will certainly pick each quote of chapters and verses everywhere each afar. About this concept, here is what it quotes from the bible which by prophet Isaiah: (*Isaiah 28:10*.) *"For precept must be upon precept, precept upon precept, line upon line, here a little, there a little."* (*2 Timothy 3:16*). **"All scripture is given by inspiration of God". And also the similar idea is quoted in the book of revelation which revealed by John the revelatory. (*Revelation 1:8*.) I am Alpha and Omega, beginning and the ending, said the Lord, which is, and which was, and which is to come, the Almighty. (*Revelation 22:13*.) I am Alpha and Omega, the beginning and the end, the first and the last.** Likewise, every scientific knowledge proves are not that easily be sequenced for derivation, but the most ideas will be proven through the perception and concise study of the Biological Sciences in nature thereafter. That is where our biologists and other scientists related are in the better avenues to prove from the scientific researches and experiments. There are no scientific experimental proves in the book of bible since it gives out the general knowledge in broad. Wherefore, the question is; does the Lord God conduct the literal researches and experiments to prove the Sciences' experimental processes as the scientists do? Does his scientific analytical proves be written in the bible precisely and consciously? Certainly the answer is not in scientific analysis. But the answers are wrapped in the broad and general topics of Biology and other sciences related through doing an empiricism researches findings. The every biblical information on biological sciences is written in a form as the key terms or parts of texts so that the certain human being may figure them out.

The Lord God's image on earth with the potentials is human being (scientists) which himself created that can conduct researches and experiments that himself had given/granted them the dominion, power, rulership, potential and authority that quoted in the book of Genesis.***Genesis 1:26*** .*And God said; Let us make man in our image, after our likeness: and let them have dominion over the fish of the seas, and over the fowls of the air, and over the cattle, and over all earth, and over every creeping thing that crept upon the earth.) (**Genesis 1:28**). And God bless them, and God said unto them, be fruitful, and multiply, and replenish the earth, and subdue it: and have dominion over the fish of sea and over the fowl of the air, and over every living thing that move upon the earth.)*

By then there some groups of people are the potential scientists which can conduct researches and do scientific experiments may prove the scientific knowledge. The others may the theologians and the bible scholars, and the other lot are those whom are inspired by the spirit of the Lord God may prove the biological perspectives are impacted for biblical purposes.

OREX JOB K. KOMBEA

PREFACE

This is a novel book, and it contains the mysterious information. It is written an informative and explanatory story about how the concepts for the book of bible in the most and entirely integrated to the knowledge for the biological science. It is the theoretical book and it explains the Biological science knowledge from the Biblical knowledge.

By then, when you view it carefully on how the biology works, it fulfils most of the bible informative texts and stories. The whole approach of biology is the knowledge of bible that will quote adequate reliable sufficient evidences with their references. The science of the biology is no difference than philosophical science of bible. And logically it proves that the knowledge of the biological science is incompliances to bible that proves how God works. The quotes of scriptures will be used from all versions.

Into this world, there we have distinguished varieties of societal religions with beliefs to prove what god each doctrinal religion serves is just and must. Into Christian religion we have come to believe God that served by Abraham, Isaacs, Jacob, Moses and the other past godly people is real and true by studying the nature of Science into Biology empiricism. I for one viewed and studied the nature of biology that proves the word of God in the bible. That is when this book is titled the Biological perspectives are impacted for the Biblical purposes.

There are some other areas of science like Chemistry, Physics, Geology, Anthropology, Astronomy and others may have their own proves whether real or unreal the notional researched into Biblical from Biological. Eventually this book will help you understand who you are in the holistic approaches. Interactively it utilizes into the integral human development – physically fit, spiritually fit, intellectually fit for the whole being into biological approaches into biblical purpose.

On the other token, this book is mostly focused on how the human body systems work in accordance with the words of God in the bible. And even other existing biological elements will come into exist to suit and match most of the godly words from the human biology because the holy bible always emphasises about holistic approaches of human being. Humanity is categorised into main triune; body, soul, and spirit for the divinity.

While being a body, we need to work (all lives on earth for working). The living creatures have to accomplish the full purpose which God created for. The foremost purpose that God created human beings is the worshiping creature. Human being has to worship God as the major and important part of his/her life span. That is where human beings shall inherit the kingdom of heaven after spirit departs from flesh, which spirit shall return to where it originated from, that is heaven (***Isaiah 66:1***. *Heaven is my throne, and earth is my footstool)* above where God is. And flesh will return to where it originated from which is dust the ground (soil) itself. Since from the biological study, upon the death of all animals – they will always lay face downwards (facing to the surface of ground). Even though, most birds fly in the atmospheric air for all their lifespan, but once they die, they usually lay face downwards to the surface of ground. So it implies that both the flesh and the spirit of the animals/beasts go into the ground and end as they don't have life-giving spirit. God had not put his spirit inside them, *(**Genesis 2:19**)*. But for the mankind, throughout the global world, the dead flesh will always be laid face upwards (facial view facing sky/heaven) in the grave. (Human dead body with coffin or without coffin, it always lays faced to the sky/heaven).

*(**1 Corinthians 15: 21**. For just as death came by means of a man, in the same way the rising from death comes by means of man. **1 Corinthians 15:42**. This is how it will be when the dead are raised to life. When the body is buried it is mortal; when raised, it will be immortal. **1 Corinthians 15:44**. When buried, it is a physical body; when raised, it will be a spiritual body. There is, of course a physical body, so there has to be a spiritual body.)*

Into that biblical concept, biologically it indicates that the flesh returns to dust (soil) which it was created from, and the spirit returns to where it comes from which is God, *(**Genesis 2:7**)*.

Therefore, every mankind shall always be buried as the face and the whole body anteriorly facing the sky/heaven regardless of distinguished cultural religions and beliefs which some believe as the Lord God who created heaven and earth does not exist.

The key focussed areas to look on

* Birth
* Human being
* Love
* Blood
* Sun/Solar
* Soil
* Water
* Work/Toil
* Air/ Breath
* Animal/Beast
* Fish/Water Monster
* Bird/Fowl
* Snake/Serpent
* Insects/Creeping Thin
* Herbs
* Hazard/Disaster

* Fire
* Light
* Enemy/Foe
* The worship of the Creations
* The Organ Head
* Reproduction
* Contend
* Food/Nutrition
* Sleep/Rest
* Disease
* Hedonism
* The Two are better than One
* Small gods
* Friendship/Allie
* Season/Timing
* Death/Cease/Extinct

The content knowledge of Biology

The fundamental meaning of the word 'Biology' is again divided into two different terms meaning to each other: **BIO** and **LOGY**, the '**BIO**' denotes "life" and the '**LOGY**' denotes "study". The term biology is of the **LIVES STUDIES**. Rather, generally it is a study of living things on earth with its surroundings like the climate and the weather, soil, lithosphere, hydrosphere, sunlight and atmosphere (gases) as the contributing factors as the platforms for biology to function its cause. In other words it is the study of the general, specific and scientific knowledge of the fauna and flora of every region or country on earth for the whole Science knowledge approaches. The specific scientific knowledge about the biology is set for deeper and broader into sophisticated knowledge. The Biologists or the scientists of biological science have different scenarios to study biology into analytical knowledge like biochemistry, biogeography and biophysics and others. They have proven the facts with all critical concepts from the scientific experiments and researches. The Biology is divided into the animal classification and plant classification (fauna and flora) with their surroundings like water, soil, oxygen, climate that play the sophisticated significant role as the contributing factors. Meanwhile but certainly biology is further divided or classified into four major groups **'Plants, Microbes, Insects and Animals. Yet the botany is divided into two major classes known the flowering and the non-flowering plants.**

The Animal /Beast Classification

The table below consist the examples of the classes of animals with their specific consisting animals:

Mammal	Reptile	Amphibian	Bird	Fish
human being	snake	toad	cassowary	shark
giraffe	lizard	salamander	wagtail	dolphin
tiger	turtle	frog	hornbill	cod
elephant	crocodile	caecilian	cockatoo	marlin
cat	tortoise	newts	parrot	eel

The Plant Classification (Botany)

Apart from the many examples, there are few that are common. The table below consist the examples of classes of plants with their specific consisting plants:

Flower-ing plants	Conifers	Mosses and Liverworts	Fungi	Algae	Fern
pawpaw	pine	shrubs	ground mush-room	planktons	Maiden-hair fern
sugar cane	cedars	adelanthacea e	Mil-dews	chara	Tree fern
kunai grass	douglas firs	Brevian-thaceae	moulds	fucus	Bird's nest fern
bread fruit	cypresses	calomniaceae	rust	tuberosa	Common polypody

sweet potato	junipers	daltoniaceae	Tree mushroom	laminaria	Ostrich fern

The Insect Classification

The table below consist the examples of the classes of specified insects

Water insect	Space insect	Soil insect	Plant insect
water beetle	mosquito	earth worm	caterpillar
tadpole	mot	ant	grasshopper
water caterpillar	butterfly	centipede	prey mantis
water Leeds	flies	cricket	bee

The Micro- organism /Microbes Classification (Microbiology)

The table below consists of the examples for the specified microbes.

Fresh and salt water micro-organisms	Plant micro-organisms	People and animal micro-organisms	Soil micro-organisms
protozoa	parasites	germ	bacteria
phytoplankton	bacteria	virus	decomposers
cyan bacteria	archaea	parasites	nematodes

| rotifers | eukaryotes | scabies | fungi |
| vibrios | protists | measles | actinomycetes |

The Geography

Mostly, the Natural Geography is the significant flat form from which the biology to perform its cause. There, it is a vital aspect that plays the diverse role as given the support to the biology. It is the general Geography on the planet earth which comprises with other universal elements like the solar systems. The Natural Geographic Science information is very significant flat forms for biology that categorised into the major realms namely the **Lithosphere**, the **Atmosphere**, the **Hydrosphere**, the **Biosphere**. They play differ roles each interactively to balance the planet earth to serve and fulfil the biological perspectives for the biblical purposes through lives in each benchmark.

The Lithosphere consist all forms of rocks. The Atmosphere consist all forms of gases. The Hydrosphere consist all forms of liquids. The Biosphere consist all forms of living things. The interactions among the spheres make intra specific relations for the planet earth. They depend on each other for the betterment for the physical earth for all lives to exist, and for biology to fulfil its cause to integrating the biblical knowledge. And from each of the spheres is derivations of sophisticated knowledge, that they come into various specific disciplines like most of the engineering fields and the different science knowledge. Moreover, it is the study of all physical and natural elements of whole universe that serves the purposes and interests of biological life on earth to fulfil the understanding of someone who is the source of life which is God.

The Sun

The knowledge about Sun is very diverse and we will look at its basics. Sun is one of the hottest spotted stars that the earth orbits as other seven planets. The earth evolves the sun for twenty-four hours and fifty-six minutes to make a complete revolution. The other planets also orbit the sun too. They have their own certain time to make a complete revolution, too. Perhaps, a study from the astronauts and known scientists like the biologists and the botanists prove and indicate that the sources of lives on earth come from the sun. The beamed ultraviolet rays of the sun cast across the many millions of miles. The ozone layer of the atmosphere is like a blanket that soaks most of the heat from the sun. The distance from the sun to earth is one hundred and forty-nine million, six hundred thousand kilometres. The earth places itself third in the planets sequence in the solar system. Other planets of the solar system capture the sunlight energy upon their distant, and vary on their sizes. The first planet of the solar system experiences the extreme hot ever.

In that manner, the global earth benefits from the sun. To the north and the south part of the earth, the temperature is extreme cold. It is due to the lack of no sun for the rest of their lifetime (both poles never experience sun; they experience far extreme least sun). That is where the very vast bergs of thick ice called pole. For that is why they are known the North and the South Polar Regions. There, the surface of the planet is parallel to the axis of rotation. The equator divides the surface into the northern and the southern hemispheres.

The castings of beamed sunrays contain ultraviolet radiation and the light energy. Ninety nine precents of the energy is reflected on earth and disappears to the earth's atmosphere in every single day. And one per cent of the energy is absorbed by earth, especially by vegetation and animals on land in every single day. The energy passes along from plants to animals in the feeding relationship namely the food web and the food chain into the various Ecosystems. Or into other scenario, human being tends the carnivore and omnivore which enables to feed on both animal and plant lives to access the energy. Sun seems the major source of the biological life on earth that fulfils what human being tends to be the top carnivore in the food feeding pyramid in order to gain energy and live as now mankind.

The sunlight energy is also being absorbed in both the saltwater and the freshwater systems, too. The sunlight is easily penetrated starting from the surface of the water to the very extreme beneath depth part of it, the water floor. The flow of the sunlight energy is like a chain in the marine ecosystem as well. Another way of the flow of the energy commences from the planktons to the small animals to the big animals to the bigger animals. Else the sunlight energy is directly absorbed in the surface of the body organs for some other motional organisms like fish, reptile and mammals.

The ultraviolet radiation of the sun light is also important for the human body. It synthesises with other food source in order to provide it with vitamin D especially for the healthy bones. The deficiency of vitamin D from the sunlight energy causes rickets in children and oesteomalacia in adult people when insufficient sunlight to their body which they do not exposed to the sunlight into rapid frequent.

The Oxygen

The oxygen is a gas. It is a chemical element with an atomic number of eight and relative atomic mass of (15.9994). Molecular oxygen (O_2) is an odourless gas at room temperature. A mixture of oxygen and other gases administered to mammals, fish, reptiles, amphibians, birds, insects, and other microscopic insects like the microorganisms/ microbes. Air consists of approximately twenty-one percent of oxygen, seventy-nine percent nitrogen, carbon dioxide zero point zero four percent and very small amounts of other inert gases like argon, hydrogen, and helium. All those known gases do other vast and vital distinguished roles to each other in order for lives to exist continually. The source of oxygen hails from mainly the plants' leaves through the chemical process called photosynthesis.

Oxygen plays significant role in animals' body, one of the vital roles done by oxygen especially inside human body is to break down digested food particles into the blood cells for its systems to function normal. Oxygen is inhaled through breathing systems called the Respiratory in the nose, pharynx, larynx, bronchi and lungs mostly by human being. Majority of the Fish class in the marine ecosystem inhale oxygen by using their organ called gills. For the microbes and the other insects, the oxygen is absorbed into their whole body.

And oxygen is always presents for the every fuel combusting (burning). For instance, oxygen is always presented in the dry wood to burn. It has many diverse uses for other purposes of life like in the hospital the health workers, and in factories provides oxygen for the specific oxygen related uses by using the complicated scientific instrumental machines. Or oxygen is very reactive gas in all chemical scientific processes and change for new substance and compounds for people and other life's sakes.

The Carbon dioxide

The fundamental study of carbon dioxide is the exhausted gas which is eliminated especially by the most chemical changes in the physical sciences. Or it is the outcome product of the most chemical reactions. Scientifically, the carbon dioxide is matter that takes up space and has mass.

The Carbon dioxide is a gas along with a few others, work like greenhouse gas, stopping heat from escaping into the space. The molecular carbon dioxide (CO_2) produces by burning fossil fuels and forests, increasing the greenhouse effect, making the earth warmer. Plants use water, carbon dioxide and sunlight to make their food (starch) in a process called photosynthesis. Plants are the living things that can make their own food by using carbon dioxide. There are also the thick and heavy carbon dioxide (smog) from the manufacturing industries and the polluted cities. This type of gas is not safe for the environment if it is directly impacted on them.

The other source of the carbon dioxide comes from the animals. The waste product of gas that released by the animals through the respiration systems, and digestive systems are taken by plants in the ecosystem in both on land and in the biodiversity. Plants give off oxygen to animals and animals give off carbon dioxide to plants. They make (symbiosis) interactions to each other for the life on earth.

The Water

The water is in the form of liquid. Three quarters of the earth is filled with water. Water comprises of any form of liquid is called the Hydrosphere in the Geography language. Liquid is like kerosene, cooking oil, salt water, crude oil, patrol and so many to be named scientifically. For the biology to exist, especially the fresh water (H_2O), and the sea water plays the precious and significant role. Seawater dominates all the sea animals and plants that they entirely depend on each other for biodiversity marine ecosystems. Food web and food chain or the feeding relationship is paramount in outnumbered in marine (underwater) ecosystems. Salt water animal and plant species cannot be transferred (adjusted) to the fresh water ecosystem; they will easily be extinct due to the distinguished climate conditions and the food types. Obviously the least animals it can be possible to adapt to the new climate and environment. But for some animals and plants can adapt the climate and environment irrespectively.

Freshwater water dominates all the freshwater animals. Likewise freshwater ecosystems cannot be adapted to the seawater ecosystems- they can easily die out due to the different climate conditions. The ecosystem in the freshwater is also effective like in shallow running waters and lakes. But there are some special water invasive species of plants and animals can be easily be adapted to different climatic environment and suit themselves into adaptation, (poikilothermic animals). Animal and plant species for the fresh steady waters like lake are bit differ from the running water due to the steadiness and flowing currents.

On the other hand, fresh water (H_2O) is vitally a significant element for people and animals to drink in order to survive. Scientifically water does very vital role in our body in different systems like in the kidneys. Moreover, water is needed for athletes when they are dehydrated. Or else we are quenching water for every time thirsting. Nevertheless, seventy-five per cent of people's body is dominated by fluid, and water is its major component. Even water is vital for the plants as their root parts absorb it from the soil for photosynthesis through the canal of xylem vessel (from the root upwards to the top of all parts of the plants). And also the water vapours in the atmosphere that cools the vegetation and animals on earth.

The Introductory knowledge of the Christian faith and the Bible

Christianity is a religion for the Christians who follow the Christ and its study is Christology. Most of the Christian nations throughout the globe were not Christian Religion oriented in the early ages and in the ancient times. Or they had not believed in Christian cultures. In the recent dates, they were influenced by the Christian philosophy, beliefs and ideologies by the early Christian Missionaries. Before the Western Imperialism of the Christian Ideologies invaded (hosted Christian crusades for renaissance by the early Christian missionaries) for the people to rebirth in the Christian faith and belief in now the Christian countries, societies, communities, and individuals in most parts of the global world. All five major races of people (Negroid Race, Caucasoid Race, Mongoloid Race, Indian Race, and Aborigine Race) throughout the world...... people have their own beliefs. That denotes; they hail from differ cultural backgrounds and belief systems that bounded into who they were, what they believed, and how they kept their customs in the simplest or complex notions in relation to what they believed and took it as their god for granted. Most of them are still practising their way of beliefs and the ritual practices. That means some people are organising their ritual activities as the religious organisations as they are current and effect. They are also spreading to other unreached places as the Christian religion is doing as its major focal and visionally mission.

The Christian religion's chief purpose is to comprehend and emphasise how Jesus' early followers, led by the Holy Spirit, spread the good news (Jesus' death and resurrection) about him in Jerusalem, in all of Judea, and Samaria and to the ends of the earth, (*Acts 1:8*). In the day of Pentecost, the Upper Room in Jerusalem, there were one hundred and twenty believers gathered prolonging prayed and worshiped. Suddenly the mighty rushing wind blew down from Heaven with the tongues of blaze toughed each one of them. The believers spoke in the different tongues the Holy Spirit enabled them to speak, (*Acts 2:1 – 13*).

In amazed, the rowdy crowd of the city of Jerusalem demanded to understand what really happened as the time was only nine o'clock in the morning, and also the believers spoke tongues in not their native language but others' languages. Peter and other apostles appealed and spoke boldly and plainly about Jesus Christ which the generations of that era came into confusion about whom he was sent by, since as the Jews religion was already existed with ceremonial laws of Moses. The crowd was convinced by Peter's message and deeply convicted. From there, upon their request "what must we do to save in the kingdom of God?" About three thousand believers had been baptised in Jesus' name without a controversy as Peter directed them, (*Acts 2: 38 – 41*). There, the whole of Christian beliefs and its ideologies had been resumed by the early Christians.That was where Christians as his followers throughout the globe and the entire world until recent.

Before that, the book of Old Testament from the Genesis to Malachi is what the people before Jesus Christ believed and lived according to its instructions. Religious practices were carried out under the dominion of God's ritual instructions which someone be the messenger as the prophets. They informed and directed people from what God had expected from the generations to generations until the time of Jesus Christ. So still the Judaism religion is only practising and living according the Old Testament lives. Christian religion lives the life by believing and practices the ritual life of both the Old and the New Testaments as long as God reveals himself in the both.

The knowledge about the book of bible

Among the various religions into this world, Christianity Religion is one of its kinds. The bible is the Book that godly perspectives are imparted to mankind. Whosoever believes and follows in them shall inherit the God's kingdom in the spiritual ram. Here is a simple acronym to help you understand the book of 'BIBLE' - Basic Instructions Believe Live Everlasting. It has broader ideas and deepest knowledge that subject to God, Jesus and the Holy Spirit. "Those three titles are one God indeed, but each performs extinguished character.

(1 John 5:7.) "For there are three that bear record in heaven, the Father, the Word, and the Holy Ghost: and these three are one". (1 Corinthian 12:6.) "There are different abilities to perform service, but same God gives ability to all for their particular service."

The book of Bible includes poetry, history, biography, philosophy, science, religion, prophesy and other inspirational writings. In particular, the book had first intensely written by wisdom oriented and scholars whom were inspired and anointed by the spirit of the Lord God. Now, there are varieties of brands written by so many authors and publishers through collecting the main ideas from the original versions. The people whom follow Christian ideologies are Christians. Study of godly notions is Theology. And the godly government is Theocratic Government System. But the Theocratic government systems are not practiced within Christian religious governments. Most of the Christian religions are governed by the Democratic Government systems. A theocratic government system is practiced especially in Islam Religion, and is particularly dominates in the country of Iran as the one for all apart from other Islamic countries. Its leader is called the Supreme Ayatollah, and after him (that power) is the president.

The certain perspectives for each segregated religions is what they have the different beliefs systems that they live as their ritual lives and granted for life. Each religion has different gods each compile with own beliefs, and ideologies that kept in their own books. Example, those books are given names like Holy Koran and their god is Allah for the Islam religion. Similar principles exert to each of the other religion entirely.

A book of Bible is written into two testaments, namely the old and the new testaments. Before that, scroll is used for all the biblical information that was written into logical and dimensional orders. In the Old Testament is from the book of Genesis to Malachi, and in it are the perspective stories before Jesus Christ, and how God dealt with generations of people starting from the creation of the heaven and the earth. The other is the New Testament. It is from the book of Mathew to Revelation. It has the culture of Jesus

Christ, and how he conducted himself into human philosophy which they would bounded into living in the ritual life. Most of the contexts for the New Testament books are referenced from the Old Testament books. Within the comprised of sixty-six books altogether, there some chapters and the verses have significant informative knowledge about the biological science those are expounded for bible purposes. The Science of it precisely manifests to fulfil the bible. What the bible quote are fulfilling the Science of Biology. Those concepts correlate to comprehensively correspond with the knowledge of Biology to make a subject 'LIFE'. Here is a simple acrostic text of the term life. **Lord integrates for everything**, according the words of God in the bible.

The Bible Testaments into sequence

Old Testament	New Testament

Genesis	Ecclesiastes	Mathew	1 Timothy
Exodus	Songs of	Mark	2 Timothy
Leviticus	Songs	Luke	Titus
Numbers	Isaiah	John	Philemon
Deuteronomy	Jeremiah	Acts	Hebrews
Joshua	Lamentations	Romans	James
Judges	Ezekiel	1 Corinthians	1 Peter
Ruth	Daniel	2 Corinthians	2 Peter
1 Samuel	Hosea	Galatians	1 John
2 Samuel	Joel	Ephesians	2 John
1 Kings	Amos	Colossians	3 John
2 Kings	Obadiah	1 Thessalonians	Jude
1 Chronicles	Jonah	2 Thessalonians	Revelation
2 Chronicles	Micah		
Ezra	Nahum		
Nehemiah	Habakkuk		
Ester	Zephaniah		
Job	Haggai		
Psalms	Zechariah		
Proverbs	Malachi		

The Commencement of the Implication on Biological Knowledge to Biblical Knowledge for each of the Content and the Key Focused Areas The Human being To identify human being into the outer perspective Biblical and Biological purpose for the notion on Human Being

Human being comes from the mammal class in the animal classification into biological concept. Human being can perform all characteristics that are performed by mammals. Human being is warm-blooded, and it cares and feeds for its young with breast milk. Human being is very wise and however is intelligent. Human being is what like other mammals but again it is superior dominating and controlling all other animals with wisdom. There is no other animal like human being. The wisdom that he lives comes from God, **Genesis 1:27-28.** *So God created human beings, making them to be like him. He created them male and female, bless them, and said, Have many children so your descendents will live all over the earth and bring it under their control. I am putting you in charge of fish, the birds, and all the wild animals.* The God of host is full of wisdom and knowledge that reigns the whole universe. Wisdom and knowledge for human beings comes from God since he i God's image.

Mainly its body is portioned into three: That is; head, abdomen, and thorax (head, body, leg). It has two fore limbs and two hind limbs. Each of the limbs portioned into three, they are foot, shin, and thigh for the hind limbs. And arm, wrist, and hand for the fore limbs. (Note: In each of the limbs and the whole body are portioned into three.) And it has three respiratory inlets; a mouth and the two nostrils. Also the five grasping fingers for each hand has three portions each. And there are five toes for each foot. The three portions similarly imply the father, the son, the holy ghost. Into the other dimensional conception it is 'Name' "GOD" for the three portions. The five fingers of each limb imply as the 'Name' "JESUS".

Into the posterior view of the face of a human being, there is something that we can look at closely, too. The organs seem letters to form words. They are like the right-hand side of the pinna (ear) that seems the capital letter 'G', and the circumference of a whole face is like capital letter 'O', and the left-hand side of the pinna (ear) seems like the capital 'D'. The two pinnae (ears) seem like the letters 'G' and 'D,' and in between them are the two eyes seem two 'O's. Also the two eyes and the nose seem as the small letter 'T'. And the two nostrils and a mouth seem also like the three breathing inlets for respiratory system. (Note: All of the parts are compiled into three). The three portions similarly imply the father, the son, the holy ghost. Into the other dimensional conception it is 'Name' "GOD". And most vitally human being operates with five senses; seeing, taste, smell, feel, and hear. Also the five common senses imply as the 'Name' "JESUS", and the face se like the 'Cross' of Jesus Christ.

Human being has a complicated language, with speech and writing. Human being makes complicated tools and makes houses and other structures. Human being invents endless machines and gadgets. Human being produces works of art such as painting, sculptures and music for pleasure rather than usefulness. Human being has many different traditions and customs passed down over the years. Human being greatly alters its surroundings, especially to grow plants and raise animals as food. Human being makes roads, factories, shops and parks, it does great damage to the environment for more than any other creature does. All these features, and many others, set it apart from other animals. Also the human being is very intelligent and wise that plays most of the common sense by knowing good and bad, wrong and right. It has moral and ethical values and set up constitutions that will guide them.

Human being is the image of God, and his likeness because of his wisdom and intelligence unlike the every other creature.

The formation of human kind

From the biblical context in the book of Genesis how God created human in the beginning. *In **Genesis 1:26-28**. Then God said, "And now we will make human beings; they will be like us and resemble us. They will have power the fish, the birds and all animals, domestic and wild, large and small", So God created human beings, making them to be like himself. He created male and female, blessed them, and said, have many children, so that your descendants will live all over the earth and bring it under their control. I am putting in charge of the fish, the birds and all the wild animals.*

__Genesis 2:7.__ Then the Lord God took some soil from the ground and formed a man out of it, he breathed life giving breath *into his nostrils and the man began to live. **Genesis 2:18.** Then the Lord God said, "It is not good for the man to live alone. I will make a suitable companion to help him. So he took some soil out from the ground and formed all the animals and all the birds. Then he brought them to the man to see what he would name them,' and that is how they all got their names. So the man named all the birds and all the animals, but not one of them was a suitable companion to help him.*

     ***Genesis 2:21-25**, Then the Lord God made the man fall into deep sleep, and while he was sleeping, he took out one of the man's ribs and closed up the flesh. He formed a woman out of the rib and brought her to him. And the man said, At last, here is one of my own kind- Bone taken from the bone, and flesh from my flesh. 'Woman' is her name because she was taken out of man. That is why a man leaves his father and mother and is united with his wife, and they become one. The man and woman were both naked, but they were not embarrassed.*

The new human life begins to form. How it forms.

To accomplish the word in ***Genesis 1:28**, human being has to be replenished, fruitful, and be multiplied. Man and woman come into one in terms of relationship: They must be the soul mates in Sexual relationships. Sex has three intimacies and solitudes involved.
1. Sex was given to propagate human race
2. Sex was given for true love within marriage
3. Sex was given so that man and woman express unity between them.
 Couple comes into deep sexual feeling on each other. The both are naked but not embarrassed and ashamed. During the sexual intercourse between them, they always feel as good as they reach into peak climax which is orgasm. Man reaches into extreme climax peak orgasm when he ejaculates semen. He deposits semen into the vagina of his soul mate, woman. Both satisfy into some extents.

What organ of the body first forms after fertilisation?

Before the embryo is formed when an egg (ovum) is fertilised by a single sperm, the zygote is the first stage of body development in the womb. However, zygote and embryo stages are heart. Fertilisation takes place in the uterine (fallopian) tube. After sperm being deposited in the vagina during sexual intercourse, sperm gradually moves up through the cervix towards the uterine tube. There are millions of sperms being deposited. Out from the millions of sperm cells when each copulation, there is only a single sperm cell fertilises the ova. Not all the sperm cells fertilised the ova. All millions of sperm move up through the cervix towards a uterine tube with the help of semen as they swim into it. After a single sperm fertilises an egg (ovum), it puts barrier as others cannot reach it. All other millions of sperms die out indeed. The dead sperms are evaporated into gas inside the uterus and then not taking longer they move out from it through as the condensed gas.

The Sperm is randomly selected to determine a gender

The millions of spurted (released) sperms during the sexual occasion is always categorised in two. They are male sperm cells, and female sperm cells. One group contains the male chromosomes (XY) while the other contains the female chromosomes (XX) with their deoxyribonucleic acid (DNA) that comprises the genetic information. Either both moves forward to meet the released ova (ova releases a time) through the help of semen. Only a single sperm cell is determined from the millions cells for the formation of the particular human being. *(Jeremiah 1:4-5. I knew you before you were conceived.)* And if the sperm cell contains the male chromosomes (XY) first meets the ova then the gender will be a male. If the sperm cell contains the female chromosomes (XX) first meets the ova then the gender will be a female. The determination of gender is from sperm but not from (ova) egg. *(**Ephesian 1:11-12**. I chose you when I planned creation.)*

The Heart is the first organ formed.

Our whole body is made of different layers, structures, and segmented parts called the organs. The body organs are both for interior and exterior views like head, forelimbs and hind limbs, abdomen, liver, pancreas, lung and others. Precisely there are more other functional organs that play the vast vital scientific roles collaboratively as the contributing factors for the whole body functioning systems. They are like lung, skeletons and kidneys, which the person can live as normal and a better healthy life.

There are eight common human bodies functional systems function interactively. Namely; the endocrine system, the muscular system, the skeletal (bone) system, the respiratory system, the dermis (skin) system, the reproductive system, the nervous system, and the digestive system. *(**Psalm 139:13**. You created every part of me; you put me together in my mother's womb.)*

Biologically, the first organ of the body that forms is heart. Cell division takes place into haploid number of chromosomes after two gametes meet. Furthermore the cells divisions take place into diploid number of chromosomes, and more divisions take place as it develops. The organ zygote is the first stage and an embryo is the second stage of the organ formation in the development of hearth. That is followed by the other stages of developments into sequence for human baby to fully mature into the womb before it is born. ***Psalm 139:14**. I praise you because I am fearfully and wonderfully made; your works are wonderful. I know that full well.*

The focal point of this area is on heart. The heart system seems the very special organ which forms as the first born of all other organ systems like brain systems, skeletal systems, and the others. Heart is like a fist of an arm, and is the central mechanisms that plays vital role in our body systems. In all stages of body development in the womb (during the pregnancy), it plays as the controlling factor which pumps as blood and expands to form other organs. It pumps out blood to all parts of the organs to make them fully develop and mature. As it pumps, all body parts develop into slow paces from phases to phases for every stage. It positions itself in the central location in the whole body so that it easily pumps and receives blood to all parts of the body.

The Heart is the controlling mechanism

The heart has its regulating systems called the conduction systems. The heart has four chambers. The upper jumpers are the right and left atria (each upper chamber is called atrium) which acts to receive blood and pumps blood into the chamber of the right and left ventricle. The right ventricle pumps blood to the lung, and the left ventricle sends blood to all other parts of the body.

The cardiovascular system is composed of the heart which acts pump, and a series of hollow tubes known as blood vessels. It is through the blood vessels that the blood is pump from heart to all parts of the body - carrying substances such as oxygen, hormones, and nutrients from digested food to all body cells. Blood returning from the body cells, contains waste products which are carried in the blood vessels to various parts of the body, example; the lungs and kidneys, to be excreted. Also into the biblical perspectives heart is the controlling factor of whole human moralities. Therefore God is always watching for the HEART. ***Matthew 5:8.*** *Bless are the pure in heart, for they will see God.*

The Cardiovascular health

- There are certain things that we can do to help keep the heart blood vessels healthy:
- Get adequate physical exercise, example; a brisk work for twenty to thirty minutes each day
- Avoid smoking
- Eat a diet which is low in saturated fats, sodium and alcohol
- Avoid become overweight and obese
- Lessen and diminish the habit of consuming the refined foods and drinks
- Eat plenty of vegetables and fruits in all meals
- Eat lean meat and whole grains
- Get practical ideas to eat for heart health in eat smart

- Be more educated from the relevant authorities and related scholars like the cardiologists and the cardio-health awareness campaigners

Given first priority to the first formed organ (Heart)

Give the first priority to the first formed organ from the body organs. According the study, heart is the first organ that forms after the fertilization of sperm and ovum. We are ought to give first preference and priority to heart which always seems the first formed. Obviously, in order for every nature to operate and exist a balanced and pretty perfect life, we can give first priority to all first formed in any means of lives. Human being has to give first priority for his/her heart. All other parts of the body are important, too.

How can we give the first priority to heart and what priorities and the essentials are to be given to it? There are major ways that we are to look at and maintain the good health and welfare areas for the heart biologically. **The Normal and Healthy Weight (Body Mass Index - BMI)**

We will always have to have a normal healthy Body Mass Index. For instance; our heart to our whole body is like a ratio 1:10 (the heart proportion to the body mass index). Once when we maintain a healthy life not having overweight and obese ball belly, we have normal and healthy ratio proportion. There, quite a maximum numbers of people whose body mass index are in normal ratio. The group of people in that category are the athletes and some who concern and maintain their bodyweight to the healthy standard.

Thus, what happens to the hearts for those who are overweight and obese? The time when the body weight increases, the hearth remains in normal capacity. It is like the ratio 1:15 or 1:20 or 1:30, it depends on how the increases of the body weight.

However, the more the weight increases the more the heart has to pump blood to all parts. Or, the higher the body mass index the greater the odds of developing high blood pressure. That is where the capacity and the potential of heart comes into weaker and stops to pump blood to all parts of the body. Gradually the whole heart resulted to fatal and leads to death for the whole body. That is called cardiac arrest.

Throughout the global world, there are more deaths resulted to the hearth attack which is source of obesity and overweight, and lack of adequate exercise, and poor diets.

More people do not understand how to control their body mass index and live healthier. They even never know how to give priority to their heart's health which leads to heart attack. We are mostly needed to be educated for the betterment of the best healthiest heart. This kind of affliction is faced by the people in the Industrialised and Western Countries, and it is number one killer and the before cancer seems the second.

The factors that contribute towards the unhealthy Body Mass Index and obesity or ball-belly body shape

- lack of doing proper exercises for diminishing overweight
- cultural beliefs to gain weight (into some societies, people want to have dignity of 'syndrome', the over pride which they are reluctant to diminish and reduce their weight and willing to put on more weight on their body) big man – big lady syndromes.
- taking weight gaining pills
- living a hectic life (working class people have no time in leisure activities like doing exercise after formal working hours, they are always busy on the work commitments)
- people do not have time for the leisure activities.
- people go for prefer eating methods, not prepare eating methods (diet selection and control or cutting down and adding up)
- moving to and fro using vehicle in frequent often rather than walk and joke
- visiting friends and businesses by using technology (telephone, mobile phone, e-mail, and fax) rather than move physically to visit
- intake of excessive sodium and alcohol into the body
- lack of proper knowledge (being uneducated, awareness campaigns not reach them)

- eat excessive every meal (much calories in the body)
inadequate
exercise and poor diet

The gradual and overall concept behind all these ideas is to eliminate and excrete the waste and unwanted metabolised calories in the body as sweat, carbon dioxide and urine. The doing of physical body movement in any sort to the extant or not is to regulating all systems of the flesh into pretty well that leads people to healthy for longevity. Once when we metabolise those body dysfunctions ... that is where it leads to the resistance of so many lifestyle diseases too, rather than only heart diseases.

The Arteries dysfunction, (coronary) heart disease

Artery is the vessel that transports the blood to and fro the heart and all other body systems. Along the cannel of artery, there is a development of fatty plaque that restricts the blood to flow normal. It is caused by excessive fat, and the access amount of cholesterol in the body. Those excessive fatty plaques are sourced from the refined food substances (poor diet) like the saturated fats and excessive animal fats. And, at the same time people do not do physical body exercise regularly (inadequate exercise) like running or brisk walking so that the system of the blood flow through the artery can always be maintained to normal. The more brisk walk or run is the more the flexible the arteries which the blood flows in the normal pace.

For the most kids' and few matured human being's common heart-related diseases is through the arteries shrinks that blocks the blood to flow normal. It is caused by taking excessive sweats and spices due to their arteries are much tender soft, as they are too younger.

The human heart in Biblically

Human heart is the magnificent mechanism that we are to relatively consider in both the biblically and the biologically. Heart tends to play most vital and significant role which is mysterious the mankind has to be known. Heart controls the whole human life as it is the first formed organ. That means heart has confirmed by what mind thinks in all forms consciences. Heart has to verify moral and immoral, feels for the loves, feels compassion, feels for peace, feels for happiness, feels for sadness, feels for bitterness, feels for sorrow, feels for rudeness, feels for anger, feels for pride, feels aggressiveness, feels for pity, feels for tolerance, feels for angriness, feels for braveness, feels for eagerness, feel for rejoice, and many more feels. The heart is like housing for particular moral to dwell. It is all about what the mankind's qualities of livings are upon the heart's control. Heart tends to be a driver of its own to direct and drive the whole mankind conducts in his/her lifespans. After all mind is in control over heart's desires and ambitions. And it makes mind reasons out and in always in the controlling system.

Biblically, human heart is where God in the full focus. Human heart is controlled by him/her and God is always in watchful. God determines mankind through heart. ***Proverbs 17:3****. Gold and silver are tested by fire, and the person's **heart** is tested by the LORD. **Romans 12:11-12***. *Work hard and do not be lazy. Serve the LORD with the **heart** full of devotion. Let your hope keep joyful, be patient in your troubles, and pray at all times. **Mark 12:30**. **Luke 10:27***. *Love the Lord your God with all your **heart**, with all your soul, with your entire mind, and with all strength. **Romans 5:5***. *This hope does not disappoint us, for God has poured out his love into our **hearts** by means of Holy Spirit, who is God's gift to us. **Mathew 5:8***. *Blessed are the pure in **heart**: for they shall see God.*

There are more several other biblical quotes that can be used for verifying about how God deals with human heart for his sake. The health of heart has to be maintained to date into both the biblical and the biological context because it is the central and the master controller organ. Too, it is the first-organ-formed part of a body so its welfare has to be prioritised by doing appropriate exercises, and biologically by eating organic foods which God himself created in the Garden of Eden, least or not the refined foods. Also the vacuum of heart must always be filled with love, peace and joy for better life in the both contexts for the purposeful being. Both the ritual and physical health of the heart can always be in central and preferential since it is the first composed organ, and God's dwelling suit.***1 Corinthians 3:16***. *Don't you know that you yourselves are God's temple and God's Spirit lives in you?* Above the most and for all,

the consequences of the heart are always to determine.***Proverbs 4:23***
. Above all else, guard your heart, for it is the wellspring of life.

Through examining the text regarding the notion on heart, there are no distinguished conceptions. The Biological perspectives are expounded for the Biblical purposes.

(***Romans 8:28***. *We know that in all things God works for good with those who love him, those whom he has called according to his* **purpose.**)

The Organ Head

The head is the part of a body of animal-class or human being which contains the brain, mouth, and main sense organs. Within a head is brain that has the magnificent controlling centre of the central nervous system located in the skull which is responsible for memory, cognition, emotion, attention, action and perception. The neurobiology is the study of brain with its function and operations especially. Neurologists have more knowledge on and apply study into it. The psychological way of living is how and where the mind functions in every conduct. Both the human being and the animal-class use brain in operating lives to exist. That means the power of life is control by head.

The application of both the Biblical and the Biological contexts using the brain by animal-class is low compared to the human being. Human being is more intelligent than animal since he/she is God's image and yet he/she the small god *(Genesis 1:27).* God has given more wisdom to human being as they are innovative, creative, talented, skilful, knowledgeable, and others. Most of all, human being is 'man'... that comes from God which he/she accomplishes godly life the 'praise' and 'worship' being with the righteousness. Human being is worshiping creature. But the most animals are more perfect than human being. Human being uses head by doing most things which are prohibited by scriptural bible those are regarded as the inequities. That means, human being creates and commits sin. The word 'Human' comes from the term 'Humble or Humiliation'. But the human being does not put that (humiliation) into practical action which is submission to God by doing away with inequities. ***James 4:7***. *So then, submit yourselves to God. Resist the Devil, and he will run away from you.*

Animal-class is the humble minded which they use their heads to live in accordance with the nature. They live the innocent life by proving their rights in the most cases. They live according the nature ... suit their environment by performing the meaningful courses and accomplishing purposes. One of the interesting things that is performed by the animals is 'minding' their own business. They do not interfere to each other until there are reasons like for ecosystem competition.

The human being has power and dominion so as he/she use mind in right purpose omitting the immoral behaviours and inequities. After all animals will not inherit the kingdom of heaven since they are not God's images, but the mankind who is righteous in the sights of God. ***2 Peter 3:13***. *But in keeping with his promise we are looking forward to a new heaven and a new earth, the home of rightness.*

The Water

How water is important to play its purposes in both the Biblical and the Biological contents to suit the common goals for lives on earth.

Into both the biological and biblical context, there are quite sufficient adequate reliable references that are to prove what the subjected element 'water' does to help humankind, and the other living things on earth throughout the entire global world. For the biblical references, there are some quotes from the bible chapters with their verses; shall be from both in the old and the new testaments. And, for the biological references, there are some derivations of knowledge into the physical waters. The information below is the correlative unified information the biblical to biological which they will come up with understanding for the common purpose for life. The symbiosis (interactions) between water, animals and plant is what mankind urges to get life.

The Biological purpose for notion on Water
The Water for life
1. **The Water for its habitants**

The one-third of the global earth is covered by water; it is an inhabitation of all diverse marine life ecosystems. Water provides the shelter and food for all dependent marine animals. The water plants like seaweeds also depend on water. The flowing waters and sitting lakes dominate most plant and animal species lives too. They provide the life for their inhabitants
.

2. The Water for the vegetation (plants) on land

Soil is watered by rain water so that all vegetation shall collect water from the ground/soil. Almost all water needed by majority plants is collected from the root parts of them using root-hairs. And the leaves, the trunks, and the branches just collect least water from rain and humidity. Water with other essential nutrients from the soil is transferred to all parts of plants using the canal called xylem vessel. And the canal called phloem vessel is used to transfer other nutrients like sunlight energy and carbon dioxide from the leaves and all the way down to the roots. All vegetations are cooled off by humidity, and watered by dew from the snow and mostly watered by rain water.

The Water plays amazed role to save the lives of plants to live as normal life.

3. The Water for human beings:

Water is important for our body, In biological measure; people need to take eight glasses of clean water daily. Without water we would die within three to four days. Water is also obtained from the foods and fluids we take. Fluid makes up seventy-five percent of body weight. The percentage of water varies depending on the person's age and amount of fat in the body. Water is necessary for everybody functions. Water is presented for the body in the following areas:

- Inside all the cells
- outside the cells in the tissue spaces
- In the blood (the major component of blood is water)
- In the brain, and surrounding the brain and spinal cord
- In the eye ball in two separate chambers
- Within the joint spaces

- In all the secretions of the body such as tears, juices from the intestines used for digesting food, urine from the kidneys, and faeces.

And the clean fresh water is needed for the two body kidneys' services.

- We quench the thirst for water after eating plenty of food, and during the dehydration in the sun or in the times of sports/athletic and exercise.

The Water plays amaze role inside human body to give life.

4. The Water for other uses

Water is essential to remove the dirt off the human body. And it is useful to wash off all dirties where necessary; like for the household cleaning. It is also useful to flush off all tracts and channels. On the other side, water is significantly vital for other purposes like in technical works in buildings, mechanical, civil and many others that suits to support the lives of especially human beings. Water can also be also significant factor that contributes in all refining, processing and manufacturing within all industrial hubs, and useful in sanitations and irrigation purposes. Another very big impact that plays by water is producing hydroelectric city that supplies the power energy to whole certain location like in the bigger cities.

Water ought to play a significant role to save the human lives.

5. Water for animal classes, insects on land

All animals and plants need water for everyday living. Water is a component of nutrition so that their whole body can function normal. Most of the animals take water directly using their mouth, and some take water from the food they eat. All insects take water from the food they take.

The Biblical purpose for the notion on Water
Water for life

1. *Genesis 7:1-24*

In the time of Noah, the human wickedness was very worse and God opened all the flood gates of heaven, and all the outlets of the vast body of water beneath the earth) burst open. The water destroyed

34

the human generation with plants and animals. And, at the same water saved Noah and his family. Also, water saved all pairs (male and female) of all plants and animals species which Noah gathered them into the Ark which God instructed to build. Water played very amazed role as to save the lives, and also destroyed and killed the lives.

2. *Exodus 14:1-13*
From the Israelites' departure in Egypt, one of the the drastic hurdles and the vast challenges apart from the cruel slavery from the Egyptian government was the water of Red Sea. It was one of the barriers that obscured the way-out for the Israelites to flee from the Egyptian army. Israites were very troubled and frightened. They complained to Moses and Aaron for what if the Egyptians army might kill them near the sea. Then, from the the leadership of Moses, God instructed him to hoist his walking-rod to dodge the water. By then, there was the great deep red sea divided itself and the Isradlites walked through on the ground to move on the other side safely. But the Egyptian soldiers with their horses were destroyed and killed by the water. Water played amazing role as to save the lives of the whole Israel population, and destroyed and killed the lives of Egyptian Armies.

3. *Matthew 3 :13-17, Mark 1:19-11, Luke 3:21-22*
John the Baptist spent ages preaching the importance of confessing of inequities and demanding the God's forgiveness. He baptised Jesus in the River Jordan. Water had to save the lives of people and Jesus Christ.

4. *Acts 2:38-41*
In the day of Penticost, the key figured apostle; Peter, preached boldly about who Jesus Christ, that had crucified by the Roman Soldiers, which the constitutional laws of Jews misunderstood him of he was blasphemously accused the Jews Religious Constitutions. Peter's message convicted the rowdy crowd of Jerusalem which they had amazed of the message and believed. Three thousand people had baptised in Jesus' name without the public controversy which inorder for them to have eternal life upon their request as where they might be saved in the kingdom of God. They had baptised

inorder for their inequities to be removed and filled with the holy ghost, and to have the eternal life. Water gave life to people. *Mark 16 :16, Acts 19:4, Matthew 20:22-23, Matthew 21:25, Mark 10:38-39, Luke 12:50, Romans 6:4, 1 Peter 3:21, John 3:5*

Jesus spent times preaching plainly about how mankind has to save by water from baptism (be borne again of water; the religious Nicodemus the teacher of the law). After Jesus' mission, the apostles also noticed the significance of water baptism and baptised the early Christians in Jesus' name. As the people to be repented, be baptised and the sins be forgiven, and be filled with the holy ghost, be lived holy life and to inherit the eternal kingdom of God spiritually. The present situational life is what we are to obey the instructions from the Bible of water baptism in Jesus' name like the early prominent godly Christian apostles as Peter and the others whom created legacy of benchmark. Therefore, the whole idea about the gospel had been preached is; repentance, baptise in Jesus' name, remission of sins by God, fill with the holy ghost from God, and live a holy life for the final call from God for eternal life. Water ought to play the significant role to save the lives especially the mankind.

The acrostic of water in human being for biblical baptism perspective is; **'WATER - Washes away transgressions everyone registers.**

Through examining the dual sets of the texts regarding the notion on water, there are no distinguished conceptions. The Biological perspectives are impacted for the Biblical purposes.

(*Romans 8:28*. *We know that in all things God works for good with those who love him, those whom he has called according to his* **purpose.**)

The Blood

How blood is important to play its purposes into both the Biblical and the Biological contents to suit the common goals for lives on earth.

The Biological purpose for the notion on Blood
The Blood is life

Blood is the form of red sticky liquid which is vital flowing in the body system of mankind that coveys nutrients, oxygen and carbon dioxide in all internal body parts. Blood is pumped by heart into the blood vessels and then carries to all tissues of the body. Many diseases can be identified by testing the blood. In vertebrates, it is coloured red by **haemoglobin**, is conveyed by arteries and veins, and is pumped by the heart and usually generated in bone marrow.

The Blood group

The blood of human being is classified into four groups – **A, B, O,** and **AB**. The blood group **O** is the universal donator to other blood groups. That means it can be transfused itself to other blood groups **A, B, AB,** and **O** to the recipient from the donor.

Blood makes up eight percent of the total body weight for human beings. Blood has many important functions. It

- Transports oxygen from the lungs to the body cells
- Transport the carbon dioxide from the body cell to the lungs to be breathed out
- Carries nutrients from the digestive tracts to the body cells

. Carries wastes from the cells, example; to the kidneys to be excreted in the urine

- Carries secretions (hormones) from the endocrine glands to the body cells
- Helps to regulate the body temperature
- Prevents bleeding through its ability to clot when there is injury
- Fight infection via the white blood cells

The Blood components

The blood consists of **platelets, red cells, white cells,** and **plasma.** Each of the components does differ works to each other. **Plasma** does containing minerals, many organic and inorganic iron, proteins, fats, glucose, hormones, enzymes, dissolves oxygen and carbon dioxide. **Red blood cells** contain the important substance called **haemoglobin**; their functions are to take up oxygen from the lungs and to carry this oxygen to all the cells of the body; and to take back carbon dioxide to the lung. **White blood cells** protect our body against invasion of anti-bodies like virus, bacteria, parasites, and any other alien

The Healthy Blood

For the formation of the red blood cells and the haemoglobin the following substances are essential:

- Protein because haemoglobin contains the protein globin
- Iron which is an important part of haemoglobin
- Vitamin B12
- Folic acid
- Vitamin C

The health of the blood can be maintained. If there is less number of red blood cells in the blood becomes less than normal, or the haemoglobin concentration in the red cells is lowered, the condition is known as **anaemia**. The causes of anaemia are in loss of blood, deficiency of iron, folic acid in the dark green leafy food, or vitamin B12.

The Blood for the other living creatures

Most animals, especially the vertebrate animals have the sticky red fluid containing haemoglobin which is pumped by the heart into the blood vessels and then carried to all tissues of the body. Each animal has different percentage of blood makes up the total body weight. They have their blood components function too. Like the white blood cell is the defence that fights against the antibodies that are maintained to healthy living. Health of the haemoglobin is maintained by the green leafy food that they eat sourced for the iron.

The Biblical purpose for the notion on Blood

Biblically blood is one of the components of flesh which regarded important. Into the past life of the Old Testament God manifested generations how valuable and precious the blood. Even in the present life of the New Testament the blood is deemed precious and valuable since life is in blood.

Genesis 9:4. *The one thing that you must not eat meat with blood still in it; I forbid this because the life is in the blood.*

Deuteronomy 12:23, 15:23.
Only do not eat meat with blood still in it, for the life is in the blood, and you must not eat the life with the meat. Do not use the blood for food, instead pour it out on the ground like water.

Hebrews 9:19-22. *First, Moses proclaimed to the people all the commandments as set forth in the law. Then he took the blood of bulls and goats, mixed it with water and sprinkled on the book of the law and all the people. He said, This is the blood which seals the covenant that God has commanded you to obey. In the same way Moses also sprinkled the blood on the Secret Tent and over all the things used in worship. Indeed, according to the law almost everything is purified by the blood, and sins are forgiven only if blood is poured out.*

Matthew 26:28, Mark 14:24. *This is my blood, which seals God's covenant, my blood poured out for many for the forgiveness.*

Acts 17:26. *He made from one blood every nation of men to dwell on all the surface of the earth, having determined appointed seasons, and the boundaries of their dwellings.*

Hebrews 13:20-21. *God has raised fom death our Lord Jesus, who is the great shepherd of the of the sheep as the result of his blood, by which the eternal covenant is sealed.*

Hebrews 9:12-14. *When Christ went through the tent and entered once and for all into the Most Holy Place, he did not take the blood of goats and bulls to offer sacrifice, rather he took his own blood and obtained eternal salvation for us.*

Apart from other religions, Christianity has the faith in the blood of Jesus Christ. About all the ideas on blood; one of the mysterious things that mankind has to understand is the purchasing of the global human population with the blood of Jesus Christ. The gradual and the mysterious thing is this; the haemoglobin of Jesus Christ has resembled and unified to every mankind's blood on earth. The sort of Christ's crucifixion and the pouring of blood was unlikely that could performed by any other prophets, godly people from other religions. Eve not one of the other religions' gods poured the blood to purchase the global human population like Jesus Christ did.

The world comprises of various and extinguished human races, religion, tradition, culture, and lifestyles. There are four major human races on earth that we are. They are; Negroid, Caucasoid, Mongolic, and Indian. There are also minor races on earth like Aborigine. That denotes, the haemoglobin of each of these races of people is common in red pigmented colour and is unified. That is where Jesus said I purchase the world with my blood when he poured it on the cross of Calvary. (*1 Peter 1:2*). *You were chosen according to the purpose of God the father and were made a holy people by his spirit to obey Jesus Christ and purified by his blood.)* Blood is considered vital and important for mankind for both the spiritual and the physical for divine purpose.

Through examining the dual sets of the texts regarding the notion on blood, there are no distinguished conceptions. The Biological perspectives are impacted for the Biblical purposes.

(Romans 8:28. We know that in all things God works for good with those who love him, those whom he has called according to his **purpose**.)

The Sun

How sun is important to play its purposes into both the Biblical and the Biological contents to suit the common goals for lives on earth.

The Biological purpose for the notion on Sun
Sun is a source of life for earth

The sun is one of the important elements for the earth in all dilemmas. It plays the unique and dynamic key role. That is, it seems all the sources of life on earth come from it. Biologically, the beamed ultraviolet rays of the sun light contain energy cast to the earth. However, ninety-nine per cent of the light energy bounces back to the earth and disappear to the earth's atmosphere, and one per cent is absorbed by earth. Even human body absorbs the sunlight energy that source of vitamin D for the healthy bones and tooth.

How does the earth absorb the sunlight energy to help give life?
The vegetation absorbs the energy from the sun. Most forms of lives need plants for food. Plants produce food through photosynthesis, a process that occurs both at day and night. During the day, light energy from the sun casts on plants and is captured by a substance known as chlorophyll in the leaves. Using water taken up by the roots of the plant, the light energy stored in the chloroplast is transformed into another type of energy known as chemical energy. This causes the plant to produce starch (plant food) and oxygen.

How does the energy from the plant pass to human being and animal life?
The energy from the plant passes to the human being and animal through the feeding relationship called the food pyramid and food chain. Or the energy from the sun flows from the feeding relationships in the natural ecosystems. Most of the animals tend to be the top carnivores.
Also the mankind is the top carnivore, and omnivore in the energy flow. That, he has sufficient reliable energy which he can always accomplish the full purpose on earth as the dominant.

The Biblical purpose for the notion on Sun
The Biblical evaluation of the Sun's purpose to the whole universe is curiosity. What a great and magnificent how sun means to its courses.

Psalms 84:11. *For the Lord God is sun and shelter. The Lord will give grace and glory: No good things will he withhold from than that walk uprightly.*

Pslams 136:8. *The sun to rule over the day; his love is eternal. The sun will not hurt during the day.*

The sunlight energy that absorbed by the herbs (herbivores) is significantly important which the source of strength and energy for human being and for most of the animal lives on the planet earth.

The acrostic of the term: 'SUN' - The **Source utilises natures. Through examining the dual sets of the text regarding the notion on sun/solar, there are no distinguished conceptions. The Biological perspectives are impacted for the Biblical purposes.**

(***Romans 8:28***. *We know that in all things God works for good with those who love him, those whom he has called according to his* **purpose.**)

The Soil

How soil is important to play its purposes into both the Biblical and the Biological contents to suit the common goals for the lives on earth.

Soil is an unconsolidated mineral or organic material on the immediate surface of the earth serves as a natural medium for the growth of land plants. It is segmented into four layers.

The layers of soil

The top layer of soil is called top soil. It contains more humus (decayed plant and animal materials) than any other layer of soil. Humus makes the top soil rich in nutrients, which plants need to grow. Topsoil also holds most of the roots of plants. The layer beneath the topsoil is called subsoil. The subsoil is where the clays, minerals, nutrients and other substances collect. Rain water dissolves these substances as it passes through the topsoil and carries them down to the subsoil. The layer beneath the subsoil is full of rock fragments from the bedrock below. Plants, organisms and rain water break up the bedrock into rock fragment. Over times, these fragments become smaller and smaller, until they become soil. The bottom layer of soil is called bedrock. It is usually the source, or parent rock of the soil above it.

The Soil impacts for lives on earth

Soil is also one of the significant factors of the world that supports and gives live son earth like the sun and water do. Without soil there won't be lives. Mostly vegetation, especially the plants grow into soil. Soil also contains insect organisms and the other microorganisms; it percolates and stores the plants' water too. (*Ezekiel 17:8*. *It was planted in a good soil by great waters, that it might bring forth branches, and it might bear fruit that it might be a goodly vine*.).

Moreover, soil is where the people use into gain more of lives into it; doing economic activities like agriculture, forestry, mining. It is also vital for the creations of smallest to the largest scales of settlements like the towns, cities and even every other activity.

The Soil's impact on human body:

How is soil very important to play its purpose in both biological for biblical to suit the common goal for lives?
Since our body is made of dust, *(Genesis 2:7)* the LORD God *formed man of the dust of the ground, and breathed into his nostrils the breath of life, and man become living soul.*

Healthy living to live a long and ripe old age *(Genesis 6:3)* and die in the age one hundred and twenty years, and more or nearest.
How is human being going to live a long life? According the bible, *(Genesis 2:7)* our body is made of dust of the ground. So our body will return to dust from where it was originated. *(Genesis 3:19)*, *you have to work hard and sweat to make soil produce anything, until you go back to the soil from which you were formed. You were made from soil so you will become soil again.*
It is better we must be always watchful of what we take (eat) to live healthier and longer. Since our body is dust the soil, we must keenly

be careful on what food that we take. The impacts of the foods that we take into our body systems are what we are. That is why, once when we take food into 'prepared method eating' rather than 'preferred eating method' then we will live up to one hundred and twenty years or die in the ripe old age, *(Genesis 6:3).* That is the foremost healthiest live which we will live for its fullness and accomplish the purposes.

We are what we eat

There is a famous biological motto, "I am what I eat" – that implies, my body is biologically made of what kinds and types of foods that I take. For instance; if I take chicken so frequent and more often without physical body exercise, then my body will resemble as chicken. Chicken grows very fast to be matured and obese leading into an inactive lifestyle. Most people in some of the Western World and underdeveloped countries are growing very fast and develop lifestyle diseases, and aged rapidly.

Into such a conscience order for us to live a healthy and long life, we are to eat nutritious food. The nutritionist and physicians always recommend the importance of the organic food for the best health and long active living. They contain the special chemicals called photochemicals (phyto means plants and chemicals means nutrients of the plants). Into that accord, we are to eat the organic foods which are rich in nutrients. Nutritional foods are the fresh foods that come from the plants. Especially the vegetables, fruits, edible foods and herbs are the ones most healthy and nutritious.

The nutritional organic foods or the vegetables contain helpful substances called phytoestrogens, and they are useful inside all of our body systems. Each of the phytoestrogen performs distinguished, specific and various tasks and functions accordingly. That is where we live fit and active healthy life not having sicknesses, sores and diseases, and not to be led into mal body functions which leads to longevity. We shall be clearly heeded on the idea that our body was made of the dust of the ground *(Genesis 2:7, 3:19*), and we will return to dust of the soil we were made of. Even God created man and put him in the Garden of Eden for the

44

foods that they could eat, *(**Genesis 2:8-9**)*. Then the Lord God placed the man in the Garden of Eden to cultivate it and guide it, *(**Genesis 2:15**)*. For these reasons, our body can always be fed by the nutritious food from the soil (vegetables and fruits from garden). The sources of the nutrition (vitamins, mineral, salt, calcium, fibre, water, nitrogen and others) of the vegetables and other organic plant foods come from the soil. Gradually plant nutrients from the soil feed the soil human body. It resists and fights off other foreign micro bodies like virus, bacteria and germs that cause sicknesses like malaria, typhoid, pneumonia, and some others. Some lot of phytoestrogens protect the immune system by fighting off foreign biotics into our body systems. (**Humus means soil, and being means life from God. For that concept, man got the name 'human being' or in other words 'soil man' _Genesis 1:27_**). That is where the term 'DIE' acrostics for "Dust invites everyone".

The lifestyle diseases and the Unhealthy people (individuals)

In the contemporary situational lives throughout the global world, majority of the deaths are related to the rampant lifestyle diseases. Most of those lifestyle diseases are originated from the typical refined and processed kinds of foods that we take. They are like; all sorts of cancers like **colon cancer, breast cancer, prostate cancer, cervix cancer,** and **knee problem, strokes, diabetes,** heart related diseases like **coronary heart disease** and **cardio vascular diseases,** and **optic problems, brain tumours, hypertension** and **hypotension. Obesity, ball belly,** and **overweight** are also related to the consumption of refined and processed food stuffs without physical body limbering. Most of these diseases become chronic, and sometimes as epidemic and those lead to health jeopardy resulted into fatality to death. There are some more other lifestyle diseases that are to be named scientifically from above.

Throughout the entire global world each country is heavily relying on the booming economic powers. One of the areas that the countries boost their economy is through food and drink refining. From all sorts of foods and drinks being refined and process, there they add all sorts of artificial nutrients and toxic substances as the nutritional values which are not needed by the human body systems. They are like the additives of the excessive sugar, salt, fat, oil and colourings which are not match and suitable into natural organic food nutrients. (People who do consume the refined foods as their diet meals get old quickly too, and those who do not take them and eat organic foods as their diet in all meals do not get old quickly.) Perhaps, the ideas on *Genesis 3:19* are adequate for mankind to heed on. (Human body is humus soil so take organic foods which their nutrients are derived from the humus soil.) That can always master into our body systems. The humus soil (dust) feeds humus soil (dust) (The perfect balance of equation) to live a healthy and active long life to die in the ripe old age. For such an idea; acrostically the term die is; 'D.I.E' **Dust invites everyone.** Our body is biodegradable matter.

Into some societies and communities, we notice few people live healthy, long and active life from taking organic foods. They may inform you about why they do not develop and experience the lifestyle diseases, and inform you of how to avoid them.

With taking the organic foods, there we may look at another area. It is **sweat.** When God pronounced the judgement to Adam and Eve *(Genesis 3:17, 19)* *you listen to your wife and ate the fruit which I told you not to eat. Because of what you have done, the ground will be under curse, you will have to work hard all your life to make soil produce anything, until you go back to the soil from which you were formed. It will produce weeds and thorns, and you will have to eat wild plants. You were made from soil, and you will become soil again.* Since the commandment prevails, the DIE (**dust invites everyone**) is more considerable.

Into other manner inorder for people to live a healthier living is through physical body exercise or doing any form of physical body activities especially to eliminate the waste products off the body which is **sweat.** For such an idea; we may define the term for the sensitive abbreviation. Here is a simple acrostic text for the term; **'SWEAT' Serious waste ever acts terribly.** To fulfil *Genesis 3:19*, (work hard and sweat to make soil produce anything) is the very great phrase of command as law we need to consider. That means we need to eliminate (excrete) unwanted waste products in many ways into our body systems. When we do physical body activity, we remove sweat and carbon dioxide as well as metabolise the disorder body systems (burning of fats and calories). The unwanted body products are like sweat, urine, frat, carbon dioxide and faeces. By doing this as the pastime and the normal activity that has resulted to maintain the healthy and pretty long living. The waste or the unwanted products as the calories cannot be stored in the body. That will lead to ball belly, obesity and overweight, as well as getting into old quickly, and developing most of the lifestyle diseases that have been listed above.

There are many people who lead into such lifestyle of unhealthy, especially most of the working class people, and some others. They do not come to realise the importance of healthy tips. One of the tips is physical body exercise to eliminate the waste products and to metabolise calories and the disordered body systems.

Wherefore, the factors that diminish people from not doing physical body activities as exercise to live pretty and healthy life:

- Life is so hectic (prolong too busy with unlimbering work commitment like office work)
- Travelling to and fro by using machinery equipment like vehicles
- Rather to move around physically to visit, use phones and call
- Use machine to work rather than work using forelimbs or hands
- Not taken physical body exercise as leisure activity
- Not taking exercise as habit and the pastime
- The cultural barriers and beliefs prevent them from exercise life
- The religious norms prevent them from doing any form of exercise
- Competitiveness for the heavy weight and fat body built
- And some more other barriers

Failure of doing some of these things cost many lives into tender young ages. It is very sad to see into some societies people dying of very young age of those so called lifestyle diseases. God created people to accomplish the complete purpose and mission to the fullest for life on earth (**Proverbs 19:21**). But, why so many people are dying young of lifestyle diseases which are supposed to be easily tricked. Even more religious people and health workers are infected and dying in the unexpected time due to lifestyle diseases.

Into some other communities and societies people always want to gain more obesity and ball belly to have gained respect from others. This type of practice is performed in the uncivilized and the third world countries. Even, they take weight gaining pills most frequently. They master the syndrome of gaining respect and values. But they do not understand what they do. They do this regard blindly and not understanding the backfire effects. As they are affected and killed by those diseases, easily the relatives of the deceased people suspiciously blame the other innocent people from doing sorcery. And that has ignited social conflicts like the tribal war that results to destructions of properties and cost lives leads to worst law and order problems.

The Healthy People (Individuals)

There is another healthy aspect of life that we are going to look into some communities and societies. There are some groups of people who are active and live healthy life. They are the athlete bodies. The athlete people are the ones that who live pretty healthy and enjoying life very well prolonged for. We may always differentiate the athlete and non-athlete people (athletes and non-athletes). Age of the athlete is older but he/she looks very young while the body of the non-athlete older and his/her age is very younger. There is an inverse and the opposite thing happening.

Into another scenario, we figure out some lot of people in our communities and societies who consume alcohol and puff cigarette as more frequently, which resulted into getting old quickly. The smoker's age is cut to few numbers of years for his or her life expectancy. And some group of people take the refined and the process food as their staple meal get into old very quickly as well.

Another group of people who live pretty healthy are those who eat the vegetable foods, fruits and drink fresh water (the vegetarians called the vegans). Or the ones who live in rural communities do most the physical body work and eat vegetables as their staple foods live very vibrant healthy life. They live enjoyable lives even in their oldest age.

Through examining the sets of the texts regarding the notion on soil, there are no distinguished conceptions. The Biological perspectives are impacted for the Biblical purposes.
*(**Romans 8:28.** We know that in all things God works with those who love him, those whom he has called according to his **purpose.**)*

The Work for the Survival

How 'work for the survival' is important to play its purposes into both the Biblical and the Biological contents to suit the common goals for the lives on earth.
The Biblical and the Biological purpose for the Work/Toil for Survival

Do every living thing does work? Yes, living thing does work inorder to survive. If there is no effort in working then there is no food to take for survival.

The idea for working implies to every living thing. That includes both plants and animals, and also human being. Each of the living things has extinguished methods and ways of effort to get food. That is how they work for survival.

When there is no effort in working that is where there is no food to take for survival. The principle of the bible in ***Genesis 3:19***. *By the sweat of your brow you will eat your food until you return to the ground, since from it you were taken; for dust you are and to dust you will return.*

How plants work in order to live

How do plants work to get their food to live as they are. Actually plants do not take food as the animals do. Still this idea is similar with how animals work to take food into biblical purposes,

Genesis 3:19. But plants reach out their leaves and shoots to the surface to trap adequate sunlight energy and carbon dioxide while their roots (root hairs) grow to very place beneath the ground or the appropriate place where they may collect water and other minerals like salt, nitrogen, and other substances as their foods.

For instance; into some content, they are responding to stimulus for adaptation. The wild taro in the shaded canopy from the jungle grows its leaves broader to collect sufficient sunlight. Colourless and tender youngest plants respond to the sunlight as their shoots pointed to it if they sprout or germinate in the shaded regions. (They sustain green pigment 'chloroplast' after they reach the sunlight for photosynthesis.) And the desert plants like cactus grows longest roots to extract water further beneath underground. Also the many other plants randomly adapt to their preferred environment to sustain their livelihoods into distinguished manner.

How animals work in order to live

For the animals apart from human being, they do not plant food but they always move all over to look for food. That means many animals work very hard every time to survive. For instance; most of the ground animals dig in the soil to take soil insects, some animals like birds fly to and fro chasing for insects and feed on the tree fruits and nectars. Insects move all over where their hosts and scavengers (food) to feed on. Fewer birds and animals gather some specific seeds for food but later germinate for plants which lead to fruit bearing plant for their consumption. That is how they work rather. Fish, reptiles and amphibians always move around to look for food every time to their adapted environment as the other animals do. On the other side there are some animals feed on other animals. That means the strongest scavengers (animals) prey (feed) on the other weaker animals (hosts). Even the insects feed on other insects and animals (carrion). Sometimes the animals quarrel and brawl. Most of the times they fight each other or the weaker animals always trying to escape and flee from their enemy to survive. So the effort that they put in is their work that performed to sustain their lives resulted in working in order for fulfilling the survival purposes. Human being is what the wisdom oriented. He is very creative and intelligent than other animal creatures. That means he/she put his/her effort in working. Toil has to be derived into many dimensions. Like machinery works, head works, and limbering works. If there is no toil than there is no food. Lazy people do not eat that resulted in hunger and poverty which leads to death.The people who don't work in any form to survive create most social problems like stealing and robing resulting in the rise of death. That is where all human being has to put effort in working on one way or the other to survive. (Sweat out guts in effort of working). If less effort is imparted to do work then there is less food, and if more effort is imparted then there is more food to eat. All living things have to put effort in working every time in order for them to live a life to fulfil purpose. *(**Genesis 3:19**)*

The nutrition/food sources
How food sources are important to play their purposes into both the Biblical and Biological contents to suit the common goals for lives on earth.

Biological purpose for the notion on Food Source
Food is the common substance that has to be taken into the body through gut (alimentary canal) for the digestive systems in the body organs for all different classes of animals into the biological content. There are varieties of food sources that ought to manipulate the system in their functions from the sources that they are derived. However, in the facts of nutritional values there are different types. That means not all the food that each animal take are similar to each other. There are different nutritional values that each of the animals takes which are needed by their body capacity and systems. Not all the animals are taking the same value of nutrition. They eat differ food source to each other. So the food that is eaten by other animal is not eaten by the other. On the other side, it can be like the poisonous or ill-treated nutrition for other animals. For instance; the food nutrition that is taken by cuscus is not taken by dog, or the food nutrition that has taken by human being is not taken by cattle. That is where on the other side animals feel sick and ill when they take in the wrong thing into their body systems.

The mankind is what he develop the so called lifestyle diseases. Most of the lifestyle diseases are related to what type of foods and drinks that have been taken in without determination and care. The common lifestyle diseases are like the sorts of cancers, coronary heart disease and cardio vascular diseases, stroke, diabetes, hypertension. Discoveries of those diseases are made scientifically from especially the refined and the process foods and drinks. That is like if access sugar contained food is take into regular basis then the type of diseases has to be developed is diabetes, and if excessive amount of all the refined foods and drinks are taken regularly then all sort of cancers like blood cancer and colon cancer are likely to develop. And there are some more other diseases that are likely to develop.

On the other hand the significant idea about what the suitable food sources that work efficiently according the body's systems need are the natural vitamins and minerals. They are derived from the organic food sources, herbs and clean pure water.

The nutrition values of the food sources are what they have to be required for the human body, and the animals' body systems. There were the adequate foods/nutrients supplies that had been provided by God since beginning till the present. This has to continue for the generations to generations. The food nutrition is what we are to always consider. There also are sufficient biblical quotes which guaranteed for food nutritions should the mankind has to take.

Ephesians 5:29. *After all, no one ever hated his own body, but he feeds and cares for it.*

Genesis 1:11. Then he commanded, "Let the earth produce all kinds of plants, those that bear fruit" - and it was done.

Genesis 2:9. And out of the ground made the LORD God to grow every tree that is pleasant to the sight, and good food; the tree of life's also in the midst of the garden, and the tree of knowledge of good and evil.

Genesis 1:29. And God said, Behold, I have given you every herb bearing seed, which is upon the face of all the earth, and every tree, in which is the fruit of a tree yielding seed, to you it shall be meat.

Psalms 104:14. He makes grass for the cattle, and plants for man to cultivate - bringing fort food from the earth.

The Bible precisely emphasis that the organic foods are what God provided for mankind and animals to take. He provided green leaves and herbs. That is where the animals somehow follow instructionsn eating natural which they don't develop the lifestyle disease like mankind.

Through examining the dual sets of the texts regarding the notion on food/nutrition, there are no distinguished conceptions. The biological perspectives are impacted for the biblical purposes.

*(**Romans 8:28**. We know that in all things God works for good with those who love him, those whom he has called according to his* **purpose**.*)*

The Air/Breath

How air/breath is important to play its purposes into both the Biblical and the Biological contents to suit the common goals for lives on earth.

Biological purpose for the notion on Air/Breath
Air/Breath is life
Air/breath plays vital roles as others like food and water do.
Air/breath is in a form of gas which cannot be seen with our physical naked eyes that we respire (breathe in and out by using the organ called lungs). Within the forms of gases, people inhale fresh gas (oxygen) apart from other common gases as smokes, and exhale carbon dioxide, this is regarded as the **air/breath**. It is important inside the human being's body systems as well as in the lives of all 5 classes of animals (mammal, bird, fish, amphibian and reptile), and the insects and microorganisms. (Fish uses gills as lungs to respire). We feel air by the wind and breeze through the movement of atmospheric air usually caused by convection and differences in air pressure.

One of the key functions that plays by **air/breath** (oxygen) inside animals' and human's body; lungs send oxygen to break the food particles in the blood and releases energy in the body systems. Likewise for every plant in all classes (flowering plants, conifers, mosses and liverworts, fungi, algae and fern) to exist and live, air (carbon dioxide) is one of the key element factors as well. For the flowering plants, carbon dioxide is a major component element with other substances as sunlight energy for the photosynthesis to take place. Mostly, people and animals can live without food and water for few days but without **air/breath** they can die in minutes.

Biblical purpose for the notion on Air /Breath
Air/Breath is life
Genesis 2:7. *Then the LORD God took some soil from the ground and form a man out of it; he breathed life giving breath into his nostrils and a man began to live.*
Job 12:10. *It is God who directs the breaths of his creatures; everyone's life is in his power.*
Isaiah 42:5. *God created the heavens and stretches them out; he gave breath to his people.*
Job 33:4. *God's spirit made me and gave me breath.*
Through examining the dual sets of the texts regarding the notion on air/breath, there are no distinguished conceptions. The Biological perspectives are impacted for the Biblical purposes.
*(**Romans 8:28**. We know that in all things God works for good with those who love him, those whom he has called according to his* **purpose**.)

The Beast/Animal
How beasts/animals are important to play their purposes into both the Biological and the Biological contents to suit the common goals for lives on earth.

Biological purpose for the notion on beasts/animals
Into the **mammal** class there are many **animals/beasts**. Most of them have four limbs, vertebral and have fur. They are warm-blooded and reproduce young for the next generations with genetics informations. They operate in five common senses. They care and feed their young with breast milk until they wean them to get old. They grow old to die and their bodies decomposed to humus/soil of

the ground. Human being takes it as the major source of protein for food. Some are domestic and some are wild. In each of the animals, there are varieties of species. Some are big while some are small. They eat different foods to each other, but few eat similar foods. Most of them are heavily relying on eating different types of plants. Grass, leafy foods and fruit foods are eaten by most of them.

Most of the domestic animals like cattle, sheep, goat, and pig are important economically. They are raised to generate the income revenue for a business ventures. They creates incomes for the entrepreneurs, and use them for other purposes and for mankind consumption.

Animals are very peaceful for themselves until they are interrupted or disturbed. They mind own business looking for food in most of their times, and looking for mating. Even they do not make barns of foods nor gather them. They do not mind how much cruel that is done by human being and other animals. Despite they never keep the terrible wrongs by human being and do not take revenge. All the wild animals always trying to flee or run away from the human being and their predators. But few of the wild beasts retaliate to human being. Sometimes the very huge monsters act as the top carnivores and kill human being and prey on them. They are like the lions, leopards, crocodiles, and the venomous snakes like anaconda, pythons, and sharks. Those monsterous animals retaliate from each other sometimes. But the human intelligence is more clever that deceive them into dominating or killing. ***Genesis 9:2.*** *All the animals, birds and fish will live in fear of you. They all placed under your power.*

One of the domestic animals that never keep the wrong doings of human being and always in very closeness to him is none other than dog. And it is very sensitive so that most of it can help human beings to hunt for wild animals. It also detects the enemy and its owner. It may perform duties when trained. It be guard and security for its owner and his/her house.

Not the most, but the least animals those are very close relate to human being are cat, pig, horse, donkey, camel, water buffalo and cattle. Most of them understand their owners and react accordingly for the better and for the bad. Sometimes they can be tamed and trained for special purposes. Like horse, donkey, camel water buffalo and cattle are the best effective land transport providers. On the other side, cattle and water buffalo are used in workforce in the agricultural industries to furrow the appropriate soil type.

Some times in genuinely they make some gestures and noises. Like they cry out during the seasons or whenever they feel hungry. And sometimes they be as the time keepers for the human beings as to when and where they make strange noises to indicate that there is an importance or a danger that somewhere around.
Biblical purpose for the notion on animals/beasts

__Genesis 1:24-25.__
Then God commanded, "Let the earth produce all kinds of animal life: domestic and wild, large and small" and it was done. So God made them all, and he was pleased with what he saw.
__Jeremaiah 27:5.__ By my great power and strength I created the world, the human beings, and all the animals that live on the earth; and I give to anyone I choose.
__Jeremaiah 27:5__. The Lord God has the concern over every animal and does what the best for them according to his likeness.
The Lord God has not put his spirit to the animals/beasts
__Ecclesiastes 3:21__. How can anyone be sure that the human spirit goes upwards while an animal's spirit goes down into the ground?
Biologically, it is easy to find in this way to evaluate in the indication conscious signs. Every living creature exists to extinct. Animals die and lay face downwards, even the bird flies its lifetime in the atmospheric air. The concept of it implies that both body and spirit of the animal go to the ground and remains on earth. But for all mankind, they die and lay face upwards. For this reason, we consciously understand that the body returns to where it originated

from (humus soil), while the spirit returns to where it originated, to God. Both the spirit and the body of animal remain on earth, while the body of mankind remains and the spirit returns to God. Too, the human being will resemble as how Jesus did. He died and buried into the tomb, but later rose from death and ascended to heaven. ***Acts1:9-10***. *After saying this, he was taken up to heaven as they watched him, and the cloud hid him from their sight. They still fix their eyes fix on the sky as he went away, when two men dressed in white suddenly stood beside them.*

Through examining the **dual** sets of texts regarding the notion on animals/ **beasts** there are no distinguished conceptions. The Biological perspectives are impacted for the Biblical purposes.

(***Romans 8:28***. *We know that in all things God works for good with those who love him, those whom he has called according to his **purpose**.*)

The Fish/Water Monsters

How fishes/sea monsters are important to play their purposes into both the Biblical and the Biological contents to suit the common goals for lives on earth.

Biological purpose for the notion on Fish/Water Monsters

Into the fish class there are multi different types of them with varieties of species. They are different to the shapes and sizes to them altogether. Like; some are dwarf, some are streamlined, and some are huge, while others are extremely tiny. They reproduce with the genetic informations. Fish lives according to the climate. Which denotes; few are freshwater inhabitants while most are saltwater inhabitants. They move around to look for food, mate and flee from their predictors. The symbiosis (interactions) is common among themselves as some for commensalism, some for mutualism and some for parasitism.

Most of them are beautiful, decorative and smooth scaled which are portrayed into attractiveness that capture the view of other fishes and animals or predators. And also the most are camouflaged to the environments like the coral reefs and weeds. There seems all are also intensively sensitive.

Fish creature is cold blooded, and most of them are classed into vertebral and chordates. The diversity of marine ecosystem is outnumbered that resulted to feeding relationships. Most of the monsterous creatures are the carnivorous as the shark species. Among the sea creatures are some others that of the mammal class. They are like species of whales, dugongs and manatees. Few are the species of sea snakes and water snakes.

Almost all fishes are wild. There is not any domestic fish. That means fish can be hardly tamed. But in some parts of the world, few people tame dolphins. Sometimes those dolphins showcase into some dramas wherein. very complicated and brilliantly with the gestures as the people tamed them to perform. On the other side, dolphin naturally has the helping sense. It rescues out the land animals whenever they are about to drawn in the sea waters from their views.

Many varieties of fishes are high sources of protein nutritionally which people tend to eat. It is the major source of Vitamin A, D. (Maintenance of healthy skin, bones and vision, and teeth, calcium metabolism). And also some of the parts of some fishes like livers, liver oil and fins are used for medicinal purposes.

People all over the world are the consumers of fish. Therefore it is demanded throughout the world. Because of that, fish plays the diverse role as to boost the economy of a particular country. There are many firms who establish fishing vessels and have refineries for fish refining and processing facilities that generate good revenue and create job employment opportunities. It is essential for global economic trade purposes.

Biblical purpose for the notion on Fish/Water Monsters
Genesis 1:20-22. *"Let the water be filled with many kinds of living beings, and let the air be filled with many birds," So God created the sea monsters, all kinds of Creatures in the water, all kinds of birds. And God was pleased with what he saw. He blessed them and told the creatures that live in the water to reproduce and to fill the sea, and told the birds to increase in number.*
Job 12:7-10. *Even birds and animals much they could teach you; ask the creature of the earth and sea for wisdom. All of them know that the LORD'S made them. It is God who directs the lives of his creatures; everyone's life is in his power.*
John 21:6. *He said, "Throw your net on the right side of the boat and you will find some." When they did, they were unable to haul the net in because of the large number of fish.* (Jesus showed the example of how Peter would win the souls.)
Matthew 15:36. *And he took the seven loaves and five fishes, and gave thanks, and brake them, and gave to his disciples to the multitude.* (Fish resembled the word of God, that would feed the multitude of souls.)
Matthew 14:19. *And he commanded the multitude to sit down on the grass, and took five loaves, and the two fishes, and looking up to heaven, he blessed, and brake, and gave the loaves to his disciples and the disciples to the multitude.* (Fish resembled the word of God, that would feed the multitude of souls.)
Fish seems the great creature that played amazing and significant role. Its purposes were awesome and wonderful. Biblically the purpose of fish tended to feed the multitude even though they seemed less in number. Likewise in the present situation fish seems to feed the multitude worldwide economically.

Through examining the dual sets of the texts regarding the notion on fish/water monster, there are no distinguished conceptions. The Biological perspectives are impacted for the Biblical purposes.

(**<u>Romans 8:28</u>**. *We know that in all things God works for good with those who love him, those whom he has called according to his* **purpose**.)

The Fowl/Bird

How Fowls/Birds are important to play their purposes into both the Biblical and the Biological contents to suit the common goals for lives on earth.

Biological purpose for the notion on Fowls/Birds

The bird is another class from the animal kingdom. There are varieties of birds with different species. Some are big, some are small and some are huge. Most of them live on ground while few live on water. Most of them fly while few walk. Few of them do not have wings. The birds do fly have the lighter bones unlike other classes of animals which enable them to do so in the earth's atmosphere.

Birds have feathers that keep their body warm. They are warm blooded and lay eggs to hatch for baby as reproduction is one of their concerned lives. They reproduce with genetic informations among each type and species. They closely look after their young and leave them until they are weaned. They have chordates and identified into vertebral class.

Birds are also the fearful creatures to other animals. They move around from one location to another to look for food, to mate, and to flee from their predators and enemies like human beings.

Almost all birds live into the jungle, forest and bush while few live in swamp, water and desert. They are the links of the inhabitant ecosystems. That means most birds are wild. They take different foods into their habitat as seeds, flowers, fruits, while majority of them feed on insects. Some birds are domestically looked after. They are like gallinaceous birds as chicken and duck.

The poultry is known for the raising of birds. The specific vital economical birds are like chicken and ducks. The raising of the economical birds into business ventures that generate the revenue of its owner in the economic reasons. The poultry can be raised by the bigger companies into the highest quantities which are beneficial to the company or the government as a whole.
On the other hand, poultry can be reserved for raising eggs. The birds are the best source of protein, and also their eggs are very healthy source of protein and other nutrients like calcium and carbohydrate.

Apart from the above information the bird are happened to play the significant activities on earth. In every single day there all species of birds play the faithful vital role as the time keepers. That denotes, like every early in the morning, all birds have to woke up and giving signal to other animals and people that the daylight for the new day. Each and every species of birds chirp into differ sounds. Some sound like singing, some like whispering, some like rattling, and all sorts of sounds they shall create. That is not only in the morning but in the afternoon and during the day-times like in the midday. In other words they act like the time keepers to ensure that there is a certain time for a particular occasion.

In most times we come to realise that there is timing for the different seasons that informed by the different specific birds. Into other extant, there are some birds inform the nature into daily basis. They ignite the signals for the weather patterns. For example; if the birds for the fine weather chirps/zips which implies that there will be a fine weather for a day, and if the birds for the rain weather chirps/zips this implies that there will be a rainy weather for a day. Also most of the birds make different chirps/zips for each timing … a particular bird chirps/zips with different tone of chirp/zip, midday

with other, and evening to other tone, and morning to other tone. The birds are the unique and best informer creatures on earth.
 Upon the study of bird; it gets its career acrostically for its name.

Biblical purpose for the notion on Bird/Fowl

__Genesis 1:20-21.__ Then God commanded, "Let the water be filled with many kinds of living beings, and let the air be filled with birds". So God created the sea monsters, all kinds of creatures that live in the water, and all kinds of birds. And God was pleased with what he saw. He blessed them all and told the creatures that live in the water to reproduce and to fill the sea, and he told the birds to increase in number.

__Genesis 8:8-12.__ Meanwhile, Noah sent out a dove to see if the water had gone down, but since the water still covered all the land, the dove did not find a place to land. It flew back to the boat, and Noah reached out and took it in. He waited another seven days and send the dove again. It returned to him in the evening with a fresh olive leaf in its beak.So Noah New that the water had gone down. Then he waited another seven days and sent out the dove once more; this time it did not come back.

__1Kings 17:2-6.__ The the LORD said to Elijah, "Leave this place and go east and hide yourself near Gherith Creek, east of Jordan. The creek will supply you with water and I have commanded ravens to bring you food there". Elijah obeyed the LORD'S command, and went and stayed by Cherith Creek. He drank water from the creek, and ravens brought him bread and meat every morning and every afternoon.

__Matthew 26:34, Mark 14:27, Luke 23:34, Luke 22:61, John 13:38.__ The rooster crowed two times inorder to fulfil what Peter would deny him three times. That was the time to verify him about one of Jesus' disciples by the servant woman of one of the highest priests when the Roman Soldiers arrested Jesus to crucify him on the cross of Calvary .

Bird seems the informing agent also in the Biblical contexts that played the inspired and the amazing roles. It plays role in the Biological world as it played in the Biblical world as it stated. Upon the study of bird, it is to be rendered acrostically for its name as;

'BIRD' - Best informer resource daily.

Through examining the dual sets of the texts regarding the notion on bird/fowl, there are no distinguished conceptions. The Biological perspectives are impacted for the Biblical purposes.

(**_Romans 8:28_**. _We know that in all things God works for good with those who love him, those whom he has called according to his_ **purpose**.)

The Serpent/Snake

How Serpent/Snake is important to play its purposes into both the Biblical and the Biological contents to suit the common goals for lives on earth.

Biological purpose for the Serpents/Snakes

Servant is name given to snake in bible. Snake is the name given in biology and it is one of the animals that come into a reptile class. Snake comes into varieties of species. Some are very vast and monstrous; some are big and long, while some are medium and small. All snakes are classed into vertebral. They are cold blooded animals. Most of the snakes have the rough scale while few have the smooth scales. Most snakes live on land and few in water, but they can adjust themselves into either of them.

Snake is like the other animals that performs the biological characters. It has sexed to reproduce, eats and excretes, move from place to place to look for food and to have mate. It operates in five senses. It fears and slithers from its predators as well as it preys on its hosts. Human being is its most enemy.

Apart from all other reptiles and animals snake has no limbs to crawl or to grasp things. Instead it slithers for movement by using its tummy. Few snakes are adapting in climbing trees, and they climb stiff slopes and cliffs.

There is one of the common unique characters that perform by snakes. However, they (snakes) have nostrils but instead of using that for smelling like the other animals for common they use their tongue to smell the environment detections. For all the other animals have one tongue and use nostrils to smell breath but for it – it has forked tongues. It flicks its tongues to the air for collecting odour - causing particles that it then delivers to a sensory organ in the mouth. It has its uniqueness in smelling using tongue rather than nostrils.

Biblical purpose for the notion on Serpent/Snake

__Genesis 1:24-25.__ Then God commanded, "Let the earth produce all kinds of animal life: domestic and wild, large and small" - and it was done. So God made them all, and he was pleased with what he saw.

__Genesis 3:1-5.__ Now the snake was cunning animal that the LORD God had made. The snake asked the woman, "Did God really tell you not to eat fruit from any tree in the garden?" We may eat the fruit of any tree in the garden", the woman answered, "accept the tree in the middle of it. God told us not to eat the fruit of that tree or even touch it," if you do, you will die. The snake replied, "That's not true," you will not die. God said that because he knows when you eat, you will be like God and know what is good and what is bad."

Snake is bit differ from other animals through its tongue. It has forked tongue. It does not keep it inside its mouth, but instead flicks out to the space in most frequent in every moment. Biologically snake uses its tongue to smell the environment while other animals use their nostrils. For this sense, biblically (*__Genesis 3:13-15__*) we have to analyse that snake was used by Satan to deceive Eve of being picking the fruit from the prohibited tree from God in the Garden of Eden. That is where it indicates that **snake** reveals truth and untruth manifesting its forked and dual tongues to the environment that informs both liar and truth simultaneously. It is also dangerous when it bites the heel of human being that spurts its venoms as he or she may dies and or impacted in some hurting measures. Because for its character and behaviour; it gets its name snake. The acrostic of snake: 'SNAKE' - Satan's networks anyhow knock everytime. Into such a sense that is where the source of all sins is disobedience since Eve started it from disobeying God's instructions in the Garden of Eden.

Obviously snake be a lier even under the control of devil. If mankind has to reveal the truth and the lie at the same time then it implies that he immitiates flickering the forked tongue. Wherefore there is a warning message from the bible to godly mankind about revealing truth and lie simultaneously. Wherefore a part-time Christian cannot defeat the full-time Satan.

Through examining the dual sets of the texts regarding the notion on snake/servant, there are no distinguished conceptions. The Biological perspectives are impacted for the Biblical purposes.

(**Romans 8:28**. *We know that in all things God works for good with those who love him, those whom he has called according to his* **purpose.**)

The Creeping things/Insects`

How creeping things/insects are important to play their purposes into both the Biblical and the Biological content to suit the common goals for lives on earth.

Biological purpose for the notion on Creeping Things/Insects

Creeping thing is name given in bible about the biological name insect. Insect is basically defines as the small animals. But it is different from animals by having fluid instead of blood, has no meat and muscle, and has no bones. There are different varieties of insects with the distinguished species among themselves in multiples. There are land insects and water insects. Some fly, some creep on land while some inside soil. Few of the insects operate in five senses while most operate in not full. Most insects are very tiny and small.

Insects mate and reproduce young with the genetic information. Almost all of them give birth through laying eggs. Some insects fly, some creep, few slighter, while few hope. They move from place to place looking for food, and to make mate, and flee from their scavengers. Also they are the worst scavengers too on the other side to their hosts.

Scientifically we can realise that there are most insects that have very vital and brilliant characters as they play the diverse significant role into their habitats in the ecosystems.

Most of them play four major roles into their surrounding habitats.

1. Each of the species of insect make different sounds indicating time, like in the morning, in the midday, and in the afternoon. For example; throughout the world there are many people whom are notified in the times for insects and respond promptly as they make sounds, or sometimes there are certain insects make sounds for the distinguished seasons like in indicating winter or summer. The flying insect named cicada is a common agent-insect that makes the sensation sound in the early morning for a day, and late afternoon for a night.

2. Into the other scientific analysis there are some other lots of the flying insects like bee and the other few creeping insects like weevils and tiny katydid species are the agents of cross-pollination (used in the vast oil-farm industries and tobacco industries for economic activities), and for the many other plants. They play as the amazing role that take the stamen (contains male sex cells) and attach to stigma for the new life to begin for most flowering plants unlike mankind do.This is very amazing that seems the mystery and episode in the understanding of the most ordinary people.

3. Earthworms and other insects are the other lot that make soil fertile for crops. Also most of them are the best food sources for some animals like the domestic pigs that become well nourished and healthy.

4. Most of the insects are as the food source for other animals (herbivores for carnivores) about the feeding relationship in the natural ecosystems, both on earth and massive vast inside marine life. One of the best and magnificent food sources that provide by one of the special insects is honey by bee. Bees in groups also provide security in some certain locations. Honey is traded whichever boosts and create economical activities. The insect wasp, the group of it can provide security by sting on people like the bees do.

And there are some other specific insects are used for some other certain purposes. Like ants are the ever busiest insects that most people learn from them to be busy for not leading into poverty and hunger.

Biblical purpose for the notion on insects/creeping things
Genesis 1:21. *Then God commanded, "Let the earth produce all kinds of animal life: domestic and wild, large and small" - and it was done. So God made all, and he was pleased with what he saw.*
Hosea 2:18. *And that day will I make a covenant for them with the beasts of the field and with the fowls of heaven, and with the creeping things of the ground: and I will break the bow and the sword and the battle out of the earth, and will make them to lie down safely.*
Psalms 104:24-30. *LORD, you have made so many things! How wise you made them all! The earth is filled with your creatures. There is the ocean, large and wide, where countless creatures live, large and small alike. The ships sail on it, and in it plays leviathan, that sea monster which you made. All of them depend on you to give them food when they need it. You give it to them, and they eat it; you provide food, and they are satisfied. When you turn away, they are afraid; when you take away your breath, they die and go back to the dust from which they came. But when you give them breath, they are created; you give new life to the earth.*

The functional works and the characteristics of the insects as the acronym: INSECTS

Insects always tend the

Noble models and be

Submitted themselves into creating the distinguished

Ecosystems which are

Common for

Transforming the biological

Symbiotic lives.

Through examining the dual sets of the texts regarding the notion on insects/creeping things, there are no distinguished conceptions. The Biological perspectives are impacted for the Biblical purposes.

(**_Romans 8:28_**. _We know that in all things God works for good with those whom he has called according to his_ **purpose**.)

The Herbs

How Herbs are important to play their purposes into both the Biblical and the Biblical contents to suit the common goals for lives on earth.

Biological purpose for the notion on Herbs

Herb is a name given to the plants which have the special purpose. Most of the herbs are derived from the wild plants like trees and vines. It is commonly used for cure diseases from body. There are varieties of plants species that are selected for herbs.

In most places throughout the world, there are many ordinary people identifying some plants as the herbs. The herbs are taken from both big and small plants specifically. They use herb for quite other reasons like for the ritual purposes too. The parts of the plants that are used as herbs are like roots, leaves, fruits, juice, skins and flowers.

However, herbs are important that they contain phytochemicals (plant chemical) like the food plants have. Those phytochemicals are essential for human body systems, and for all plant eating animals. The phytochemical is divided into varieties of specific chemical substances like phytoestrogens for preventing cancers and other lifestyle diseases. Also within those phytochemicals, there are more varieties of other chemical substances also presented. They act as the antibiotics and the body-system cleansing substance.

That is why those people who take herbs frequently live pretty healthy life and unlikely to develop the lifestyle diseases. The very good example that we ought to look at is the animals. The animals shall not feel sick and never one time present themselves to the clinics for medication. The reason behind that is their body systems are functioned by the phytochemicals since they are heavily relying on eating plants (herbivorous), especially grasses and leafy plants. Within their body systems are functioned by the herbs.

Scientifically, botanists and physicians study different plants to ensure making medications. Eventually most of the medical drugs are made from the herbal plants. Since then we can recommend the herb plants as vital substances in our body systems.
Vegetables and fruits are another means of herbs. All plant foods that we take are herbs. The people whom do away not eating animals products and feed on plant based food are vegans. Those people are also known the herbivores and vegetarians. There is very much interesting thing that you will come to realise is the vegetarian people. The physical views of their body is very unique compared to

flesh and meat eaters. That means; their body skins are very smooth and shine, they are slim and look tall, they are so muscular, they do not grow grey hair until to the very ripe old age, the skins of the body are not wrinkle in rapid pace, the faces are not wrinkle in rapid pace, they do not develop all sorts of lifestyle diseases. They are the very smartest and healthiest human beings on earth. Male looks much handsome and woman looks much prettiest. And they are very smartest thinking people and knowledgeable, and do not develop mental disabilities as they are very brilliant intellectually.

Biblical purpose for the notion on Herbs

Genesis 1:11-12. *And God said let the earth bring fort grass, the herb yielding seed, and the fruit tree yielding fruit after its kind, whose seed is in it, upon earth: and it was so. And earth brought fort grass and herb yielding seed after its kind, and the tree yielding fruit, whose seed was in it after its kind: and God saw it was so good.*

Genesis 3:18. *It will produce weeds and thorns, and you will have to eat wild plants.*

Genesis 9:3. *Now you can eat them as well as green plants; I give them all to you for food.*

Hebrews 6:7. *God blesses the soil which drinks in the rain that often falls on it and which grows herbs that are useful to those for whom it is cultivated.*

Those people whom are self-proclaimed health gurus who talk about a holistic approach between health, food and religious are the wise people that we would notice. Biblically, in the book of ***Daniel 1:12-17, 20,*** tells us the story about that motive applied by Daniel and his three friends from the tribe of Judah in the royal court in Babylon for the King Nebuchadnezzar's kingdom after the LORD let him captured Jerusalem from the king of Jehoiakim belongs to the tribe of Judah.

Daniel 1:12-17*. "Test us for ten days," he said. Give us vegetables to eat and water to drink. Then compare us with the young men who are eating the food of the royal court, and base decision on how we look. He agreed to let them try it for ten days. When the time was up, they look healthier and stronger than all those who had been eating* *the royal food. So from then on the guard let them continue to eat vegetables instead of what the king provided. God gave them four young men knowledge and skill in literature and philosophy. In addition, he gave Daniel skill in interpreting visions and dreams.* **Daniel 1:20**. *No matter what question the king asked or what problem he raised, these four knew ten times more than any other fortune-teller or magician in his whole kingdom.*

Here is a simple acronym has to be understood about the term 'HERBS' - Healthy eating runs body systematically. Through examining the dual sets of the texts regarding the notion on herb, there are no distinguished conceptions. The Biological perspectives are impacted for the Biblical purposes.
*(**Romans 8:28**. We know that in all things God works for good with those who love him, those whom he has called according to his* **purpose.**)

The Hazards/Disasters

How Hazards/Disasters are important to play their purposes into both the Biblical and the Biological contents to suit the common goals for lives on earth.

Biological purpose for the notion on Hazards/Disasters

The term destruction is a name given to Disaster or Hazard into the biogeography ideology. So hazard comes into two categories. They are Natural Hazard and Manmade Hazard. The impacts of the hazards are to kill and destroy both natural and human environments (biological lives on earth) into massive quantity and devastating.

There are many hazards that can be identified to name. They are like; tsunamis, earth quake, flood, landslide, volcano, hurricane, hailstorm, bushfire, war, explosive dynamite, explosive bomb, drought (el Niño), epidemic diseases, thunder, mudslide, cyclone, over crazing, glacier, arson (fire), frost, storm (Lal Niño), hunger and poverty, out breaking pandemic diseases, and more to name.

All these hazards are very dangerous. They have their own causes that hardly control by man. For instance; flood is caused by down pour of heavy rainfall, most of the tsunamis are caused by the giant sea waves that are triggered in the submarine earth quakes, and few are also caused by the landslides taken underwater. And draught is caused by prolong sun. Rest of all the other hazards have their causes too. Even the manmade hazards have their causes.

Rapidly all the natural hazards caused the destructive effects that mankind cannot control. Manmade hazards can be controlled into some measures, however. Some of the destructions that they cause are devastating which cost the people (government) vast sums of money, effort and time to restore and recover in their normalcy.

Biblical purpose for the notion on Hazard/Disaster

Genesis 6,7. *The massive rain flood destroyed the whole world in Noah's term.*
When the people had spread all over the world, the LORD saw how wicked everyone was on earth and how evil their thoughts were at all times, and violent had spread everywhere. Everyone was living evil. The LORD found no fault in Noah. God saved him in the Ark with his family and the selective plants and the animal species while the whole world had jeopardized and fragile by the flood from the downpour of massive rainfall within the fourty days.
Genesis 19:1-29. *The furnace fire destroyed Sodom and Gomorrah in Lot's term.*
The LORD had not found even the one tent of the population of Sodom and Gomorrah with no fault and guilt. All of their men lived homosexual and gay lifestyle. The inequity were peak and had paramount. Only Lot lived faultless and God saved him with his two daughters. The LORD God destroyed the two cities with furnace sulphur.

Exodus 14:27-28. *So Moses held out his hand over the sea, and at the day break the water returned to its normal level. The Egyptian soldiers tried to to flee and wanted to run away from the water, but the LORD threw them back into the sea. The water returned and covered the chariots, the drivers, and all the Egyptian army that had followed the Isradlites into the sea; not one of them was left.*

By studying of the disasters in any means of destructions costing the people's lives and properties, we can realise that God's anger reveals. God stroke the peoples where they lived inequity in the past. God had not come directly in the form of physical image to kill and destroy them but uses the natures to cause the **hazards/disasters**. There are also the similar situations that happen in the present times where there are inequities. ***Proverbs 10:29.*** *The way of the LORD is a refuge for the righteous, but it is the destructions of those who do evil.* ***Deuteronomy 26:61***. *The LORD will also bring on you every kind of sickness and disaster not recorded in this book of the Law, until you are destroyed.*

Through examining the dual sets of the texts regarding the idea on hazard/disaster, there are no distinguished conceptions. The Biological perspectives are impacted for the Biblical purposes.

(***Romans 8:28***. *We know that in all things God works for good with those who love him, those whom he has called according to his* **purpose.**)

The season

How seasons are important to play their purposes into both the Biblical and Biological contents to suit the common goals for lives on earth.

There are four major seasons which are divisionally taken place in every year. They are spring, winter, summer and autumn. There are some things particularly happen within each season. All of these seasons have the major biological implications in lives on earth. The lives are determined by the seasons and they are adapting to them. All of those seasons bring fort good and the bad impacts. Into other means the season comprises of any means the naturally set-time for their occurrences. **_Genesis 8:22_**. *As long as the world exists, there will be a time for planting and a time for harvest. There will always be a cold and heat, summer and winter, day and night.*

In other words, season is a part of every year when something particularly happens; like rainy season, **(_Leviticus 26:4_**. *I will send you rain in its season and the ground will yield its crops and the trees of the field their fruit.*), fruit season, nut season, mushroom season, dry season on weather, season of particular season of insects, and the others too. There is an appointed time for everything. **_Genesis 1:14_**. *And God said, "Let there be light in the expanse of the sky to separate the day from night, and let them serve as signs to mark seasons and days and years.* Human being and the animals are well aware of each season. The seasons are the environment influential which they (human being and animals) adapt themselves or cooperate accordingly. Some species enjoy while other suffer. This means each seasons are good or bad for each of them. Preferably on the other side we will have taken it as the timings. Everything has their own timing for their causes nevertheless. As timing for making love, timing for birth, timing for die, timing for planting and for harvest, timing for mourn and timing for laughter. To everything there is a timing which we have to experience and live as life. **_Ecclesiastes 3:1_**. *To everything there is a season, and a time to every purpose under the heaven.*
Through examining the text regarding the notion on season, there are no distinguished conceptions. The biological perspectives are impacted for the biblical purposes.

(_Romans 8:22_. *We know that in all things God works for good with those who love him, those whom he has called according to his* **purpose.)**

The Light

How light is important to play its purposes into both the Biblical and the Biological contents to suit the common goals for lives on earth.

Light seems the source of all illuminations. Light is one of the flat forms that the biology has to perform its cause for the biblical purpose. The paramount source of light is the natural medium emanates from the sun. There are some other sources of lights that contribute towards the notions on biological to biblical purposes. ***Genesis 1:3***. *And God said, let there be light: and there was light.* ***Genesis 1:4***. *And God saw light, that it was good: and God divided the light from the darkness.* ***Genesis 1:5***. *And God called the light Day, and the darkness he called Night. And the evening and morning were the first day.* ***Genesis 1:14***. *And God said, let there be lights in the expanse of the sky to separate the day from the night, and let them serve as signs to mark seasons and days and years.* ***Genesis 1:15***. *And let them be lights in the expanse of the sky to give light on earth. And it was so.* ***Genesis 1:16***. *God made two great lights – the greater light to govern the day and the lesser light to govern the night. He also made the stars.* ***Genesis 1:17***. *God set them in the expanse of the sky to give the light on the earth,* ***Genesis 1:18***. *To govern the day and night, and separate light from darkness. And God saw that it was good.*

There are two groups of biological practices and activities. One has to be done in light while the other in darkness. Almost all biological practices are done in the time of light. That means; light provides its energy to all plants for photosynthesis from the sunlight. The animals/beasts that move around in the daylight to feed on foods mate, and their minds work effectively for the other daylight activities. Bird does most of its causes in the daylight; they chirp/zip, mate, feed, and compete while other animals do their cause both in the dark and in the light. Insects are other lots that most of them perform their causes in the lights, too.

Also light has the greatest impacts on human's lives. He/She performs massive and most of the toil/work in the daylight. The mankind uses light to moves around places to places, sees and recognizes things by differentiating them, uses daylights to count the number of days, uses light to determine the effort put in a particular thing, uses light to do godly and spiritual performances, uses daylight to identify the different weather patterns, uses daylight to dry up wets, and there are so many. Even he/she uses other lights to use for the causes to be done and to make analysis and determinations upon the conditions and the systems operates.

Biblically, light is used for the spiritual or mental illumination (supply with light) which enlightens the useful information. Therefore there are certainly many of them. The term light can be rarely used for the biblical purpose. Meanwhile it is used for the parables quotes. For instance; the scriptures imparted in the lives of people are like the light imparted into the darkness. The death and the resurrection of the Lord Jesus Christ is good news to the world abroad. And the humanity's repentance and anticipate Jesus Christ as the personal Lord and the saviour is like a light as it paves and wipes the thorough darkness into their lives. (***John 9:5***. *As long as I am in the world, I am the light of the World.*)

Through examining the texts regarding the notion on light, there are no distinguished conceptions. The Biological perspectives are expounded for the Biblical purposes.

(***Romans 8:28***. *We know that in all things God works for good with those who love him, those whom he has called according to his* **purpose.**)

The Disease and the Sickness

Disease is the name given in general condition for the abnormal of the body cause dysfunctions and discomforts. Biologically, diseases are varieties and most of them are divided into two major categories. They are the **Communicable Diseases** and the **Incommunicable Diseases**. The communicable diseases are ones that are infectious and they are like malaria, tuberculosis, HIV & AIDS, whooping cough, and more others. They are transmitted from person to person or from animal to human being and vice versa in some cases. The incommunicable diseases are the ones that not passing from person to person in most cases and more of them are known to be the lifestyle diseases. They are like diabetes, cardiovascular diseases, stroke, hypertension, all sorts of cancers (accept mouth cancer), optic and vision problems, arthritis and more others. They are all chronic diseases which lead to death. Some of those diseases like coronary heart diseases are severe and leads to fatal death which is really miserable.

Throughout the world, diseases are the number one threat in human's life apart from others. To suit that, every individuals experience sick/ill in diseases from its varieties. Those diseases kill millions of people every year in total. That means the highest percentage rate of death is related to diseases. Every disease has its cause and it has been discovered biologically by the physicians and the medical researchers using the complex and sophisticated machines. Most of those diseases are curable by dosing with the antibiotics and other medicines which are scientifically invented by the expert medical doctors and physicians. Most of those diseases are cured by taking herbal foods. They can also be prevented through the faith in the means of religious wises. Meanwhile a number of the lifestyle diseases are cured through changing the lifestyle system most especially by diet controls and physical body exercises. There, massive efforts are put in health organisation systems because the name disease is the number one killer for the human population globally.

Biblically, into the similar manner of understanding how diseases are affecting human life is in the biological context of its cause. A disease to human being is one of the harsh penalties that are rendered by God from the human being's inequities. The Lord God rendered severe penalties to the people whom are disobedient and ignorant in what God himself expects. That is where God punished most people in the past.

Exodus 15:26. *He said, "If you listen carefully to the voice of the LORD your God and do what is right in his eyes, if you pay attention to his commands and keep all his decrees, I will not bring on you any of the diseases I brought on the Egyptians, for I am the LORD, who heals you."* ***Deuteronomy 7:15***. *The LORD will keep you free from every disease. He will not inflict on you the horrible diseases you knew in Egypt, but he will inflict them on all who hate you.* ***Deuteronomy 28:58-59***. *If you not carefully follow all the*

words of this law, which are written in this book, and do not revere this glorious and awesome name -- the LORD your God -- the LORD will send fearful plagues on your descents, harsh and prolonged disasters, and severe and lingering illnesses.
Deuteronomy 28:61*. The LORD will also bring on you every kind of sickness and disaster not recorded in the book of the Law, until you are destroyed.*

The contemporary epidemic disease that rapidly sinks and combats the global population growth is none other than HIV & AIDS. It has no cure in all means as the relevant scientists hardly discover any. Even they have exhausted avenue to look for its cure source. The cause of this disease is sourced through the human fornication (it spreads by sexual intercourse not within marriages which is ethically unlawful and immoral). *The anger of the LORD arose when Sodom and Gomorrah had lived a homosexuality that was immoral life.* ***Genesis 19: 1-29****.* The wilful gay life practised was fully intense in peak. Wherefore the two cities of Sodom and Gomorrah were under the ruin of furnaced sulphur from God. There is an intimacy involves which is slightly biblical in these paragraphs of contexts. Diseases and sicknesses can also be infected in people's lives on the other way tactically. Almost maximum numbers of insane people are in the good health even though they are psychologically and intellectually affected. This implies that, their hygiene is extremely poor for more of them. Even most of them feed on garbage and waste, and perished and ruined food stuffs. Even they do not maintain their nutritional meals either. They live on the deteriorated hygiene conditions. They rest and sleep on streets without body coverings from the insects bites like the mosquito that infect with the diseases like malaria. But you will not notice them in the clinics because they are sick from the unhygienic lifestyle and from the unhealthy eating habits. The very mysterious motive behind it is that; they commit sin no more. That means, they do not commit these known inequities as argue, gossip, covet, jealous, steal, fight, worry, think a lot, robe and some of the immoral and unacceptable behaviours and deeds like the normal wisdom oriented, clever, scholars, brilliant people. Sometimes they (the insane people) do mistakes but they do not mean what they do because their cognition (mindsets) are already in the intellectually and psychologically turmoil. Yes, on the other dimension we take them as they are possess by devil, but remember; they do not commit inequities wilfully, but commit sin meaninglessly. (Note: They do not robe large sums of money as the white collar criminals, lies in laws like the lawyers, be thieves like the accountants, to be like criminals to robe the financial institutions, wilfully causing the terrorist network activities, blasphemous as the religious people, rape and murder, make plotting, and few to name. These types of offences are committed by the intellectual and cognitional-able people.)

All kinds of the diseases we name are belongs to the sane and the normal people, the brilliants, the wisdom oriented people, the clever people, the scholars and the intelligent people. (Most of those diseases are the chronic lifestyle diseases.) Those types of people are the ones that commit inequity since their mind capabilities are function in the normalcy. As they are intellectually deflected, they commit sin through worry, covet, steal, robe, loot, gossip, ignorance, fight, gamble, homosexuality, fornicate, adultery and more others. Sometimes those types of people are the ones that live a mingle life. Because of those consciences, they are infected by the diseases so you will easily notice such people visit clinical areas and pharmaceutical zones rarely and frequently for treatments. They will be treated to cure even though but after all the diseases will again affect them because they continue to live the inequity lifestyle and always align and intact with an immoral life. Sometimes the type of disease cannot be identified into the body by physician that causes ill to people.

God strikes people with severe (heavy and terrible) penalties through diseases if they are continuous ignorant and disobedient. The life of a particulars person has a calling for his purpose but when he or she is keeping on sinning, that is when God's anger arises. The essence of calling can be in the religious ministerial duties, or it shall be in the life of God's fullness. (***Hebrews 12:5-6***) *My child; pay attention when the Lord corrects you, and do not be discouraged when he rebukes you. Because the Lord corrects everyone he loves, and punishes everyone he accept as his child.*

The character of the Lord is merciful; love of him has no boundary to the mankind regardless of whoever they are in their afflictions. Obviously two of the quotes from the book of Mathew are deemed paramount into these approaches which are still in effect for the current and the contemporary into the humanity. *(Mathew 4:23-24) And Jesus went about all Galilee, teaching in their synagogues, and preaching the gospel of the kingdom, and healing all manner of sickness and all manners of disease among the people. News about him spread all over Syria, and people brought him all who were ill with various diseases, those suffering severe pain, the demon-possessed, those having seizures, and the paralysed, he healed them.*

Mankind can be saved from the grace of God through repentance, and live the life according his likeness and purpose. The name that above all names, power above all powers, the miraculous name, sign and wonder working name, the name that saves the whole world, the name that every knee bows, every tongue confesses, the name that the devil and the demons tremble, and the name that every disease cures and the illnesses heal, Jesus Christ is the name. This name is what most human kind believes to live the healthy lifestyle throughout his/her lifetime.

Through examining the sets of texts regarding the notion on diseases and sicknesses, there are no distinguished conceptions. The Biological perspectives are impacted for the Biblical purposes.

The Hedonism way of Life

Hedonism way of life is one of the meaningful concepts in life that human being has to understand. Hedonism has to be considered for what it becomes as the major norms for him/her to live a normal and pretty healthy life. What is hedonism? It is the highest way of pleasure and happiness in mind and heart which someone beliefs that will enable as the highest good and vital part of life. Hedonism way of life for human being is what most of them do not come to understand. That is where they do live the meaningless lives. Hedonism is all about happiness for lives that human being has to handle for his/her lifelong. Once when they apply the way of hedonism into their lives which is where they bring forth either ease or peace for happiness in lives.

Most of the human beings live asceticism life as they deny the feeling of happiness. Even they do not bliss and cheer in the times of the occasions like party or in the achievements. They substitute it into other moods and moral of feeling like worry, anger, unhappiness, stressfulness and loneliness. Those types of moods and morals of live take human beings into more problematic lives. The problems are like unidentified rarely sicknesses, mental disorders, high blood pressure, hunger and poverty, financial constraints, religious and spiritual life distractions, social disorders, family problems, and so many others and it becomes more worse and worse. All those moods are bad and they can lead human beings to unexpected lifestyles. Sometimes those types of moods kill human being. *Ecclesiastes 3:12-13*. *So I realise that all we can do is to be happy and do the best we can while we are still alive. All of us should eat and drink and enjoy what we work for. It is God's gift.*

Some human beings are brilliant and clever by understanding what it means by hedonism. They always manage the lives of the asceticism through overcoming them. They compel to live a healthy, happy and positive life by overcoming all odds despite the constraint circumstances. There are some intellectual beings and philosophers understand the life of hedonism and asceticism. Therefore, they come to write or quote the wise, amazing and inspirational sayings, statements, articles and stories to capture the moods and the morals of human being for proverb lives so that they may examine and live them accordingly. Most human beings are driven by the proverb lives and they live a prosperous happy hedonism life. *Philippians 4:4*. *May you always be joyful in the union with the Lord. I say it again: rejoice! Ecclesiastes 5:19-20. If God gives us wealth and property and let us enjoy them, we should be grateful and enjoy what we have worked for. It is a gift from God. Since God has allowed us to be happy, we will not worry too much about how short life is. 1 Thessalonians 5:16-18. Be joyful always, pray at all time and be thankful in the circumstances. This is what God wants from you in your life in union with Christ Jesus.*

The hedonism way of live can also be identified within the animal kingdom meaningfully. There are quite high numbers of animal classes who live the hedonism life. Naturally they do have sense of asceticism. That means they fight or quarrel among themselves competitively for various reasons. Even though most of them fight or quarrel into some sense like for the environmental competitions and their asceticism arose for the negative moods. But they do not have the sense of keeping the wrong doings of others for prolong. That is the very deflected worthy and beautiful sense of manner. They maintain to live the enjoying and happy lives minding own concentrations. Even, they do not live worried lives. In this sense in the lives of animals, they do not mind about their future. They do not concern about their tomorrow. Even they do not bother about past. This implies that they do not even store food and concentrate for future like the human being does.

One of the classical animals that live the way of hedonism life is dogs in mammal class and the birds. The other side of dog's life is unique and captures the mood of interest of the viewers and examiners especially the human beings. Dog understands its owner very well. It keeps to stay close with him/her, and have a sense of others are not its owners. It has no sense of keeping the wrong doings of its owner for abusing it. It is always the happiest mammal who wags its tail, indicating happiness and that is very unique trait for it. Most birds do not stay close with human beings or other animals until they are tamed. They feel enemy none but they take risk from the dangers of the surroundings. Most of them are the happiest ones which sing lovely songs (chirping/zipping) to their environments as creating the harmonious and wonderful echoing sounds.

Through examining the sets of texts regarding the notion on the hedonism way of life, there are no distinguished conceptions. The Biological perspectives are impacted for the Biblical purposes.

(**Romans 8:28**. *We know that in all things God works for good with those who love him, those whom he has called according to his* **purpose**.

The Contend

The idea contends is the main stream fight seems the way of conflict in quarrel or in abuse. It can either be single or war. Contend is one of the tussles that bring fort dangers and destructions into lives and their surroundings. It has a massive negative impact that also brings social unrest in human societies in most areas. Fight has ignited and commences off from various extinguished causes and reasons.

The fight can be verbal, physical action and through thought. From the humanity the sources of most fights are always started from covet and jealous as it commenced in the spiritual world in heaven. **Revelation 12:7-9** *Then war broke out in heaven. Michael and his angels fought against the dragon, which fought back with his angels; but the dragon was defeated, and he and his angels were not allowed to stay in heaven any longer. The huge dragon was thrown out – that ancient serpent, named the Devil, or Satan, that deceived the whole world. He was thrown down to earth, and all his angels with him.*

The idea of fight is an inheritance way of spiritual contend which sparked in heaven is one of the figured biblical contexts. It started off when Lucifer the spiritual music leader angel in heaven whom had committed sin (the angel Lucifer covet in thought over God of what if he be God and the angels may worship him) against God. There was very vast dispute and the great controversy in heaven. God had casted him down to earth with the one-quarter of angels whom were the back benchers of Satan. **Isiah 14:12-14** *King of Babylon, bright morning star, you have fallen from heaven! You were determined to climb up to heaven and to place your throne above the highest stars. You thought you would sit like a king on that mountain in the north where the gods assemble. You said you would climb the tops of the clouds and be like the Almighty.* Sin was first commenced in heaven before in the Garden of Eden by Eve and then by Adam. The acronym of the term sin: **SIN - Satan's Intelligent Network.** Therefore a part-time Christian cannot defeat the full-time Satan. **1 Peter 5:8.** *Be self-controlled and alert.*

Your enemy the devil prowls around like a roaring lion looking for someone to devour.

Also covet had begun from the first human generation, the two wright brothers Abel and Cain. So the covet and fight between, and among the siblings is not that mistake because it started from the blood line and it has to be inherited from generation to generation. Cain had murdered his brother Abel for jealous and covet of the competition on the food offering to God. The story has quoted in the book of ***Genesis 4:2-8.***

The trait of quarrel is the way of inequities. We regard it as the devil's deceived toil which is unacceptable manner in human lives. But the contends are always between one person to another, within a family, clan to clan, tribe to tribe, country to country, and others since it is one of the devil's highest ranking departments. The impacts of contend is dangerous and costly, and it is regarded as threat and fear. It causes both the physical and the moral harms that bring divisions and disputes which fragile the spiritual values, too. The idea of contend is also applied in the animal kingdom and it has practiced. They do not have the sense of pity and compassion for other species. They only have sense for their unweaned young ones only for feeding and caring. After they have weaned they do not intensively care for them but they contribute towards population. The idea of it is applied when they compete among themselves for survival. This type of practice is performed in the animal classes. The classical kingdom where all species of animals live is inside some parts of African continent. (The animal sizes are varying from the monster to the medium to the small. They are like the species of elephant, hippopotamus, ox, water buffalo, emu, oestrus, alligator, lion, rhino and many more.) They fight seriously to defeat each other. There are some animals within mammal class seem carnivorous. The cat family is the most strongest and dangerous among all other animal species. Lion is the most hero and cunning cat which defeats others before leopard and tiger. ***Nahum 2:12***. *The lion killed enough for his cubs and strangled the prey for his mate, filling his liars with the kill and his dens with the prey.*

In the reptile group is all species of crocodile and few snakes like anaconda are carnivorous and dangerous. They assail and or contend with other animals (host) to prey. That is where they fight each other but other weaker ones flee from the strongest ones. Also there is similar situation taken place inside the marine ecosystems. There are none allies to each other but foe among each species. However, fish class dominates the kingdom whilst few others are like the reptiles and the mammals. The bigger shark fish is the most cunning predatory, and it is a strongest amongst the most. That implies the other species do not give easy hurdles to it. They contend until they flee from each other and hide or either die neither flee. Otherwise it kills them or they kill it.

 Least impacts exert in the bird class. The common hero and the top carnivorous birds are none other than osprey and eagle. They are medium in size but strong in competition and not defeated by most mammals, weaker medium fish and snakes. The other birds that are stiff and heroes are the emu, ostriches and cassowary. They are larger and tough so that they can fight with other animals effectively. Or they can escape from the other animals. They can also fight with mankind. The bird class maintains self-defence and regain stability.

Through examining the sets of the texts regarding the notion on contend, there are no distinguished conceptions. The Biological perspectives are impacted for the Biblical purposes.

(**_Romans 8:28_**. *We know that in all things God works for good with those who love him, those whom he has called according to his* **purpose.**)

The Friendship

The friendship way of life is a mutual compromise that human beings and the extinguished animal classes have in their lives accordingly. It is one of the qualities that are lived for lives. That denotes; friendship brings fort some kind of manner traits in kindness as peace and harmony, love and compassion, share and fairness, grace and mercy, care and guide, pity and concern, assistance and helpful, and more others. Almost most of these traits are characterised by human beings. **1 John 4:7.** *Dear friends, let us*

love one another, because love comes from God. Whoever loves is a
child of God and knows God.

Through the careful study the moral traits on animals are what they
performed by most animals in each class does. The bible does not
emphasise the casualties on the friendship in animals among
themselves. Those traits will be clearly identified in some extent.
The mutualism idea of practices in the ecosystem is what known to
be the best idea of fairness. For instance; the mutualism symbiosis
(interactions) between pig and wagtail bird… wagtail bird feeds on
the parasites (louse) from the pig. It is mutual accord. Each of them
benefited from each other as the bird feeds from the pig to satisfy its
hunger while the pig reliefs from the harm of parasites on its body
skin. (It is like; you grab my bag, and I grab your bag.) This type of
friendship is fairness, and the idea on sharing.

There are other types of friendship traits apart from mutualism are
performed by other distinguished and the various species of animals.
That means they keep and uphold love even though cannibalism and
carnivorous acts prevail. Some differ animals are friendly and care
for each other. Most birds leave foods feeding zones as others may
take. On the other hand they indirectly care for others by igniting the
warnings of the dangers that may alarm from the nature or from the
enemies. Furthermore as the similar way they become as the security
to each other. Other unclosed related animals also maintain the
relations since they share the same ecosystem which they get to
know each other throughout their lifespan. Sometimes the tamed and
the domesticated animals even become friends in some senses if
they share common environment.

Dolphin in the seawater ecosystem is the best helping agent and
friendly for the land animals. It has a clear sense of rescuing the land
animals whenever they are about to drawn. Even it fights against
other fish that want to prey on them. Human being is what most
likely that given helps by dolphin whenever they are drawn. That is
why the dolphins are always following the sea transport machines
like the ships and ferries.

However, everything is created for purposes and they have to fulfil them in whichever that assigned.

Through examining the sets of the texts regarding the notion on friendship, there are no distinguished conceptions. The Biological perspectives are impacted for the Biblical purposes.

(**<u>Romans 8:28.</u>** *We know that in all things God works for good with those who love him, those whom he has called according to his* **purpose.**)

The Sleep/Rest

Sleep is the state of reduced consciousness during which a human or animal rest in a daily rhythm. Sleep is one of own kind for every human being and the animal class as part of life. It is another attribute that contributes towards the biological perspectives for the biblical purposes. There are some good things as the result of sleep. The sleep can be by night for the whole body rest and for to see the next day.

During sleeping there it brings fort dreams which we believe that things might come into pass. In the past the spirit of the Lord dealt with his prophets and the godly people like Joseph the son of Jacob, and Joseph the bodily father of Jesus effectively. ***<u>Mathew 1:20</u>***. *But after he had considered this, an angel of the Lord appeared to him in a dream and said, "Joseph son of David, do not be afraid to take Mary home as your wife, because what is conceived in her is from the Holy Spirit.* Even the spirit has given the dreams to the ungodly people which they believe and live it accordingly. What they did or saw in their dreams were what happen in the real physical and the material world. Most times those dreams were in parable so that they could interpret which they would come to pass. Two of the most effective and meaningful dreams that dreamt were the dreams of King Nebuchadnezzar of Babylon which had interpreted by

Daniel about the king's reign and his kingdom would be in ruined and himself be turned into beast, (written as the whole book of Daniel), and God informed Joseph the bodily father of Jesus to marry Maria when she was pregnant of Jesus which was from the holy ghost before she married with Joseph. However, the dream and the interpreted story of the King Nebuchadnezzar which revealed by Daniel,... the story in the holy bible is like prophesies, and like the parables which will happen in the future that some lot of the Christian denominations predict.

We all believe about the dreams that we have in our sleeps. We view visions when we nap. Even we have bad and scary dreams without having good sleep that resulted from day long unethical and immoral behaviours and the activities.

Sleep is part for our body system. Most of the chemical reactions and functions inside our body system are done during rest in all night-long sleep. Too, sleep sieves off every tiredness and weaknesses from the body systems and brings relief and boost strength for the next usual activities. That means the normal resting time for sleep is eight to nine hours every night. Sometimes we sleep in less time within fewer hours or in minutes and that is called nap which reliefs from the slumber. Rather sleep is what makes people or other animal class grow. Each night of the sleep makes changes to the body systems. Sleep and have a sufficient rest provides the best side of health and wellbeing. There are negative health effects when not sleep for the expected time-frame for every night.

Sleep starts from the day one of birth until death. We may always expect that the growth and the development into us are taken place every night when we rest and sleep. It is taking place in the slow pace in all body developmental phases. It had started from the youngest to the oldest. It is the natural implication and is also taken place into animal class as well. That means in every nightly sleep is aging. On the other token sleep is what we may understand the sample of death (breath is still working but consciousness is out as the eyes are closed). It is a daily death. For instance; if you are fifty years old... you die (three hundred sixty-five nights multiply fifty years equals eighteen thousand, two hundred and fifty deaths.) That includes the every nap that you have however.

Through examining the sets of texts regarding the notion of sleep, there are no distinguished conceptions. The Biological perspectives are impacted for the Biblical purposes.

(***Romans 8:28***. *We know that in all things God works for good with those who love him, those whom he has called according to his* **purpose**.)

The two are better than one in all lives: human being, animals, and plants

The ideas on two things are better than one thing is much considered. Life is better and balance when there are two things intact together. In most cases of life, there are two things combine or comprise to make one for its purpose. Life may be better for single or interested by living and existing in one. But it may not that what some of the things which has to be done within the two will not happen. For being one or single is not good idea and which there will be an unbalance life has to flow. There are some negative and the miserable impacts that are regulated and resulted from being a single. The biological world has more impact into such a life the fullest. According the biological perspectives there seems two in all aspects of lives. That denotes there are two different particulars have to come together for some common purposes. There are some key areas that we will look into these perspectives. In the most cases of life to be balanced and perfect is for the two are better than one is for male and female.***Mark 10:16***. *But from the beginning of the creation God made them male and female.*

The two are better than one, human being.

Biblically, in the book of Genesis it quotes about lives that live by human being. ***Genesis 2:18***. *And LORD God said it is not good that* *the man should be alone; I will make him a help meet for him.* There seem more areas that we are to consider according the quote. Male and female for human being is to be the soul mates for lifetime as married couple becomes one in flesh. ***Genesis 2:22****. And the rib, which the LORD God had taken from the man, made a woman, and brought her unto the man.****Genesis 2:23*** *. And Adam said; this is bone of my bone, and the flesh of my flesh: she shall be called woman, because she was taken out of man.* Since the quotes in the bible have pertained on the couple's oneness matters, it carries out the concerned responsibilities and performances that have to be considered as they are life-longing. The common areas;

- to teach and educate ritual lives and belief systems to each other, and lay foundation to the offspring for the future generations' concerns
- for being the helping agents to each other
- to being the concern partners to each other
- to reproduce offspring for the future generations
- to satisfy the sexual desire for each other
- for being the companion for each other
- to benefit relatives and dependents into some measures
- to be the security and guard to each other
- to be the helping and assisting hand for each other
- to provide warmth in the bed in the night resting for each other
- to share ideas and thoughts for its benefits and advantages

It is a great concern for the two to be as one (couple) for the idea on the two is better that one. The two means one in flesh as they bound together as single. It is like a positive and the negative impacts for the male and female in common purpose like the sexual relationship. Either of each offers one hundred per cent to each other. The reason being that they have the subject the married couple and nothing less shall break the barrier (marriage) unless spouse dies. To divorce the marriage is an immoral act which is unethical. Breaking and divorcing of marriage is one of the cultural issues into the human kingdoms. Human being has set aside constitution to deal with the conflicts arise within the marriages. Making of love or having intercourse outside the marriage and conducting fornication and committing adultery are morally unlawful that brings the justice problems. The couple may confront some extant violence but again they will come together as one afterwards.

Two can mean for one is not only for marriage. It can also mean for more than two people may be practised in common courses. People help people are what all about caring and sharing. Too, human being has the sense of understanding and reason out things which are common and shall have caused worthiness. To come together for common purpose for human lives are what all about bringing into collectively for the two or three or more for the better effects. Sometimes we may consider on the two differ groups or parties of people come mutually in understanding for assisting hands like making of trades, and providing aids and funds to each other.

Two are also better life among most animal classes also highlighted for exerted. Most of the animals act two or is into togetherness about their lives.

Two are better than one, birds

Genesis 1:21. So God created the great creatures of the sea and every living and moving thing with which the water teems, according to their kinds, and every winged bird according to each kind. And God saw that it was good. Genesis 1:22. God bless them and said, "Be fruitful and increase in number and fill the water in the seas, and let the birds increase on the earth." Apart from other animal populations, most bird species are the ones that live in pairs. The foremost common purpose for being the pair is to accomplish the word 'be fruitful and increase in number'. Most characters that performed by the groups of birds is to;

- to feed and care about their young together
- build their nest together
- chirp/zip and sing together
- signal or make alert sounds to the nature together
- take the risk of each other together

Most birds operate in the groups of three or more. The characters that performed are in groups. They move around in groups but afterwards they will still go out in twos as the pairs. Most birds biologically do not have make cloning relationships with differ birds, and have not clone within the inter-species of a particular bird family. Most bird species, especially the large ones lay two eggs during the birthing.

The two are better than one, mammal

Genesis 1:25*. And God made the beast of the earth after his kind and cattle after their kind, everything that creepeth upon the earth after his kind: and God saw it was good. . **Mark 10:6.***But from the beginning of the creation God made them male and female.* Apart from human being most of the mammals are not maintaining in the notion of 'two are better than one'. Most of the animal species do not maintain the characters that are performed by bird class and human being. One common character that performs by them is; the two (male and female) come together for mating reason. Another best thing that performs is a kingdom and creates population by coming together. However, the mothers of all animals are the ones in intense in the care and look after their young. They feed and wean them by creating differences for the competitiveness for their environment.

Similar kind of ideas on mating of mammal has applied on all other classes as the reptile, fish and amphibians (fish and amphibian do not look after their young intensively). Almost all insects intensively provide care for their eggs and young. Most of their two is better than one is for mating. The attractiveness of the opposite sex is what enables for either of them becoming into one. Wherefore, most of the classes of animals have mate, clone, do copulate anyhow, anywhere, whenever, wherever as they prefer and wish regardless of others. They are fulfilling the biological purposes through accomplishing the word in ***Genesis 1:21*** as be multiplied, fruitful and replenish.

 Human being is what in control of having copulation in the private scene in between the couple without noticing by neighbours or the others since they have sense of moral value in heart. Animal class copulate anyhow it depends. Sometimes in the eyes of human bring fort shame and dishonour when themselves enjoying by fulfilling the biological purpose. They even also have backcross sex between parents and offspring or among the offspring since they do not have the sense of moral shame which God had not put inside their hearts. Most of the mammal and bird class take up security measures. The couple in most cases collaboratively depend themselves from enemy if they can. This kind of measure is taken to protect their young ones. They also take turn to feed and guide their offspring.

The idea of being the two parties become one is also regarded in the other three (reptile, amphibian, fish) classes. The common area that they meet is in the mating times. Otherwise they do not come into one for other purposes like birds and mammals do.

Even every insect species practice of becoming one from two for mating purpose. Otherwise they do not come into one for other purposes like birds and mammals do.

The two are better than one, plant lives

Genesis 1:11-12.Then God said, "Let the land produce vegetation: seed-bearing plants and trees on the land that bear fruit with seed in it, according to their various kinds." And it was so. The land produced vegetation: plant bearing seed according to their kinds and trees bearing fruit with seed in it according to their kinds. And God saw it was so good.

The name 'two', or male and female about the plant lives are not specifically mentioned in the bible. But the quote; "Let the land produce vegetation" *Genesis 1:11-12*, is what it means about the plant reproduction that will be sprouted through the mating of two reproductive gametes in most plants, especially the seed bearing plants. Most of the germinating plants sprout from the dicotyledons while others from monocotyledon for the seed bearing plants.

The general characters for the plant lives are different than the animal lives. Apart from all other characters the trait of mating is common purpose. Actually we understand that plants do not move around to make mating. They are always stabilised in a particular location. Even they do not move around for their functional nutrition for their entire structural part components as we know and understand. Every plant's needs are provided at the location where it is by the nature as the sunlight energy, rainfall water, and nutrients from the soil.

Plants are divided into two classes in the matter of two categories for mating purpose in the reproduction discipline. One is the sexual reproduction plants while the other is the asexual reproductive plants. The sexual reproductive plants require male and female gametes to make or create new life. The asexual reproductive plants require only a single parent to create a new life.

Most of the flowering plants produce or bear the sexual gametes. The specified male gamete called sperm, and ova the female gamete which forms seeds after (fertilisation) they meet for the next generation. The acquirement is; two are better than one reason for the purposes.

The two are better than one in the human being, and the animal class' body part organs.

The bible has not mention the concept on the two anatomical and the two equal body features and structures in human being and animal class. But, certainly the hint on *Ecclesiaste 4:9-10* is relatively conscious: *Two are better than one, because they have a good return for their work: If one falls down, his friend can help him up. But pity the man who falls and has no one to help him up.* Life is unbalance and miserable when one of its two is out or off in its formal systematic operational order. If one of its two is out of operation or in disable the other left is like a survivor that is workable to accomplish its purpose to contribute for the whole body's normalcy. But, must the impediment life have to flow when there is a part offs in the operational systems. Thus, sometimes it becomes as the self-esteemed to perform its purpose not in the expected measures. If the both parts were to off for the systemic condition; they then contribute to the negative impacts to the whole body operational systems. That is the negative and the dark side of life. But the good news for them is this; most of them manage themselves to live anyhow.

The two body operating organs which make body balance to serve its purpose for human being and for most animals.

- the two equal portioned forelimbs, the arms for each animal class
- the two equal portioned hind limbs the appendage (legs) for each animal class
- the two equal wings for each bird class
- the two equal eyes for each animal class, and human being
- the two equal ears for the animal (mammal) class and human being
- the two equal testicles for each animal (mammal) class and male human being
- the two equal kidneys for each animal class and human being
- the two equal breasts for the human being, female
- the two equal nostrils for each animal class and human being
- the two equal gills for each fish class in certain
- the two equal horns each for certain animal class
- the two equal wings each for certain insect class

The common conception for why these selective organs are being the two sets is that; in the malfunctioning of either one of them, the other is picking up the roles of the both to service its purposes for the whole body. For instance; a single kidney can filter the body fluid if other is out or malfunctioning, a single testicle can produce sperm if other is out or malfunctioning. The idea of 'two is better than one' has although be imparted in other practical arena of life which suits the whole approach of Science. Lives also become interesting and purposeful when the two unequal opponents come into intact for few other living creatures. The life becomes meaningful when the two unequal concepts come into opposite to each other.

Life is balance and meaningful where there is; the positive and the negative, the good and the bad, the up and the down, the rich and the poor, the lightness and the darkness, the moral and the immoral, the good and the evil, the weak and the strong, the high and the low, the heaven and the hell, the cold and the warm, the wet and the dry, and the list goes on for the more that come into intact. Human being is one that learns the lives from the above listed perspectives. Life is meaningless and lifeless when there is no inverse and opposite of its kind for full operations.

Through examining the sets of texts regarding the notion on 'the two are better than one' in all living organisms, there are no distinguished conceptions. The Biological perspectives are impacted for the Biblical purposes.
(***Romans 8:28***. *We know that in all things God works for the good for those who love him, who have been called according to his* **purpose**.)

The Human being is small god.

The Lord God created human being on his image, and he said; this being is my image and likeness as he put his spirit inside of him.***Genesis 1:27***. *So God created man in his own image' in the image of God he created him; male and female he created them*. If human being is God's image and Godlike; then human being is another god or small god. And, the Lord God put his life-giving spirit to him/her unlike the animal lives and every other creation. This implies that the Lord God had granted the approval for all means of authorities, and all means of willpowers, and all means of dominions, and all means of potentialities, and all knowledge and wisdom upon mankind. The Lord God had placed all abilities of creativeness insite of human being so that he or she creates, invents, makes, moulds, lifts, destroys, fix, mends, analyses, conserves and modifies the creations like the human creations and the environments that which God will not. These are the creations that known to be the manmade environment which the Lord God not create or make them literally but he guides and directs into their process through wisdom and knowledge. ***Proverbs 2:6****. For the LORD gives wisdom, and from his mouth come knowledge and understanding.*

Few of the creations that (small god) man has to create or invent from the orders and authorities from God are;

-invent sophisticated machineries like devices and motor engineering equipments
-        making of new man and woman (life) through mating by copulation, cloning
-        creating the manual machines from the simplest to the complex for distinguished purposes and uses
-        creating and making clothes (fashion designs for all sizes for both genders), and designing of costumes
-        setting up settlements from the small scales to the large scales
-        setting up industries in all aspects of manufacturing, and refinery work
-        creating and modifying foods, drinks into processed and refined
-        inventing of energy system like hydroelectricity and fuel burning generators
-        making and conducting researches to come up with the knowledge and skills, and set out platforms which will be suitable for granted as the driving tool, for innovation and enhancement like for law enforcements for mankind
-        develop attitudes and exert common senses through in all aspects of lives
-        create, design and build the constructive and civil works
-        create and design the architecture and concrete structures

- breeding and producing the livestock and animals
- reserve wild lives and set up parks, and introducing cash cropping
- invent the physical science chemicals and their processes, and invent the pharmaceutical chemicals, and industrial chemicals
- to identify different diseases and able to invent medicines

Legitimately, there are more and more countless human creations that man has to create apart from God's creations like the natural environments since his orders and the authorities are prevailed. The Lord God shall not literally create the (creations) things which human beings are supposed that he has already granted authority. The Lord God had made what the heavens and the earth, and the other creations have to be.***Proverbs 3:19***. *By wisdom the LORD laid the earth's foundations, by understanding he set the heavens in place.* The general human orders are of pursuing domination, controlling and managing of all lives and surroundings. Without God's legitimate nothing human creation are to be created. Whoever the human bound those creates or invents is like a witness and the representative that fulfils the purposes of God.

The earthly world is the practical avenue for godly worship with the trait of ritual and sacred irrespective of any religion. Indeed the essence nature of the Lord God is sacredly holy and spiritual worthy. He needs all his images to be like him in worship for his glory and worthiness since in heaven is of that ambition and culture. The multitude of angels in heaven worship the Lord God in his likeness and that is the whole purpose for the Kingdom of him. ***Revelation 7:11*** . *All the angels were standing around the throne and around the elders and the four living creatures. They fell down on their faces before the throne and worship God.* Therefore the small gods are the worshiping creatures. They will spiritually align with the angels in heaven and be the worshiping gods to God after entering in it. Perhaps by fulfilling this conception every mankind has set aside religious activities as one of the major aspects of the living as it is practiced continuously. The similar type of ritual activities are also practised by various other elated religious people as they worship their gods as the living creatures.

About the living of a ritual life by worshiping and praising god is by means of fulfilling the focal purpose by every mankind. That denotes most people or the organised religious activities and spiritual societies are not belong to the one and each kind like for the Christian religion's worshiping organisations. Thus, each has distinguished belief systems that profounds for their ritual realms.

Nevertheless, the religious cultures are inheritance way of lifestyles which pass on from generations to generations. The Christian religion is whereby vast influential religion that hosts crusades in phases to phases for renaissance. Even the frequent revivals have to be taken place from time to time for uplift the standard of spiritual services. The witnessing, preaching and sharing sermons are the other ongoing key areas for winning the souls.

Through examining the sets of texts regarding the notions on the 'human being is small god', there are no distinguished conceptions. The biological perspectives are impacted for the Biblical purposes.

(***Romans 8:28***. *We know that in all things God works for the good of those who love him, who have been called according to his* **purpose**.)

The worship of God by the creations

Do we literally understand how every creation apart from human being's worship, and or serve God? The book of bible does not precisely emphasise on that knowledge. We understand that there are two common creations namely the animate and the inanimate. Yet the animate group is categorised into the animal and plant classes. The literal definition and the nature of worship for human being is by performing certain actions with raising certain tones of voices like scream and shout that sings worship and praise. Yet sharing the word of God or reading bible for collecting information and listening from the sermons. Anyway, human being is thoroughly not similar to other creations especially the animals and plants.

Plants do not make any noise or make motion by themselves until the breeze or wind blows and touch on them by other objects. There, the similar types of ideas that exerted in some of the inanimate like the water waves and the clouds, and or wind and breeze themselves.

The making of sounded noises like chirp and cry by most animal's class like birds and mammals are common. They perform different dramas and perform some activities. Some insects are the noisiest, and the drama performers, too. All those performances are taken place in the certain times of a day. Most noises like chirp of the birds are taken place in every morning and every evening for each day. Even for most insects produce noises in the morning and evening. Frogs and the toads are the ones that produce noises every night long. Even the species of different fish in all waters are the best drama performers. The other animal classes are in the similar manner.

Now, how will we understand that they make all those noises and the dramas for? What are all those produced sounds and dramas mean to other species of animals and each other natures? May be some of those characters and noises are for worshiping and praising God. There are verses in Psalms quote the critical and sensitive in the ideas about worshiping God by the creations.***Psalm 66:4***. *All the earth bows down to you; they sing praise to your name." Sellah.* ***Psalm 69:34***. *Let the heaven and earth praise him, the seas, and everything that therein.* ***Psalm 98:4***. *Make a joyful noise unto the LORD, all the earth: Make a loud noise, and rejoice, and sing praise.* The general name for earth in Psalms refers to the animal and plant creations with their surroundings. Therefore, praises and worships are always given to God almighty by earthly creations.

Through examining the dual sets of the texts regarding the notion on 'the worshiping of God almighty' by all creations, there are no distinguished conceptions. The Biological perspectives are impacted for the Biblical purposes. (***Romans 8:28***. *We know that in all things God works for the good of those who love him, who have been called according to his* **purpose.**)

The Death/**Cease**

Goodbye the beautiful and the wonderful physical world. We will never be back as we go for good. We are going back to where we were originated from. We are going because the time is due to return. The world has enough for us and we are leaving it behind. It opens the door as we go in. It is an order; none rejects it as we are all called to go. This is what the individual living organisms including human being say. Wow! What a terrible and miserable place that opens its mouth... the grave of dust? Dust invites everyone, DIE - from it we were originated. The death comes into the life of anybody anytime irrespective of how old they are.

Genesis 2:7*.The LORD God form the man from the dust of the ground and breathed into his nostrils the breath of life, and the man become a living being.* ***Genesis 3:19.*** By the *sweat of your brow you will eat your food until you return to the ground, since from it you were taken; for dust you are and to dust you will return.*

The biological existence of the earth is temporary living and, or it is not that permanent. Every living creature has a set time that will come to an end as it is known the lifespan. But the most do not reach that far as they cease or extinct in the middle. There are surplus contributing factors that diminish the life-span of all existing organism. They are like the environmental related dangers as the hazardous disasters and predators as we aware of. Rather most biological creations' lives come into short due to the human impacts on them. Otherwise they complete their lifespan, and later cease on time. Sometimes the death comes in a life of the one who is always unrighteous in any age. However, the nature of God is holy and he hates sin. He loves mankind unconditionally but hates the human's inequities and wickedness. The death creeps in the life of human from the consequence whereas. The inequity peaks as the mountain that slams resulted to death in the life of human being.***Romans 6:23****. For the wages of sin is death; but the gift of God is eternal life through Jesus Christ our Lord.* On the other view there is an advantage what the word of God in the book of bible; emphasises about sprout, replenish, and reproduce even though there is cease in the creation lives. God ordered plants to be sprouted and reproduce when he first created earth. He had also given orders to all classes of animals to reproduce, multiply and replenish the earth when he created them. For that conceptions there must always be the offspring and the new ones that replace the older and the unfit ones. That is where the lives are the ongoing existing journey from the generations to generations.

Genesis 1:11*. Then God said, "Let the land produce vegetation: seed-bearing plants and trees on the land bear fruit with seed in it, according to their various kinds." And it was so.*

Genesis 1:24*. And God said, let the earth bring forth the living creature after his kind, cattle, and creeping thing, and beast of the earth after his kind: and it was so.*

The cease or extinct occurs in every individual organisms including human being. For instance; each and every human has his/ her voice tone or fingerprint that identifies the own identity as an individual. Likewise that exerts to every other living things. For the reason being that dust invites every living creature in individual way and it returns to its original form the dust of ground.

Through examining the sets of texts regarding the notions on death/cease, there are no distinguished conceptions. The Biological perspectives are impacted for the Biological purposes.

(***Romans 8:28*** *. And we know that in all things God works for the good of those who love him, who have been called according his* **purpose**.)

SUMMARY

God is always good in our lives. His name is highly exalted and can be always cherished. Through Jesus Christ everything is answer to God and his purposes are accomplished by his images the small gods which you and me. Every creation is created and made for reasons and each has purposes. In order to fulfil that there some of us come up with creating godly research books like this one with the help of the Holy Spirit. It can be one of the contributing benchmarks in one way or the other as testimony how great God is in those who read it.

All the informations that put into this book is the remarkable explanation story of the Biological Science in the Book of Holy Bible in most, and it is the Biblical theory for researches. There are escalated essences of the Biological Science knowledge which most mankind may uncover. The Biological perspectives are impacted for the Biblical purposes. Actually there are no scientific proves that we may identify for verifications in the bible. The Biological Science in the bible is put into the general and unspecified approach into certain chapters with their verses. Even they are not aligned and sequenced in analytical orders so that they shall easily be understood by mankind. That is where the evolutionary science has more opposes on the creation science which is contradictory.

Meanwhile the related scientists are the small gods which are the images of God. They have willpower so that they can do the scientific implications for the proofs. They have come up with more proves that can suit the pertaining knowledge about the related areas. It contains the broader general knowledge in particularly the encouraging words for the humanity which God expects.

There people even are not the skillful scientists/evolutionists but their minds pop out with questions on how the biological world is biblical which doubts creep in. Also more and more Christians just only believe without some proves to verify. The idea on how this book has written for which is through the **empiricisms.** The term empiricism means the study done purely through observation and recognition of the experiences and conditions of how a particular area that takes its courses. With this concept the empiricism is taken in the Biological sciences in the Bible, and it is written. This book can become one of the contributing platforms of reference that will sought the relevant information. It will be used for verification on how the great God manifests himself to the mankind into such those ways.

THE BIBLICAL BIOLOGY